Today's parents are between a rock and a hard place. They want to protect their kids from the worst of the Internet, TV, movies, video games, and music—but they don't want to wreck their relationship with their children by always saying "no." Good thing Bob Waliszewski can show you the why and *how* of teaching your kids to make wise entertainment choices. Create your Family Entertainment Constitution and start practicing *Plugged-In Parenting*.

GARY SMALLEY
Author, *Change Your Heart, Change Your Life*

Bob Waliszewski is one of the foremost experts in the world on creating a media-safe home. This is a must read for any parent who wants to help their kids navigate the ever-changing culture and thrive. *Plugged-In Parenting* is filled with practical insight and years of wisdom. This book could be the most important investment you can make in the lives of your kids.

JIM BURNS
President, HomeWord; author of *Confident Parenting*
and *Teenology: The Art of Raising Great Teenagers*

Bob Waliszewski knows what he is talking about! He is a brilliant man with a brilliant message. Families with children need this book to protect them from the degrading media influences that plague this nation. The timing of this book could not be better!

DR. JOE WHITE
President, Kanakuk Kamps

I was six years old when my brother took me to see *The Blob*. Although tame in comparison to what passes for science fiction horror today, I had nightmares for months. In fact, I was convinced an amoeba-type alien would find his way into my tiny bedroom in Southern California! Over four decades later I still remember how those graphic scenes clouded my innocent mind. In this excellent and timely book, Bob Waliszewski provides wise counsel along with useful tools that will help parents put into practice the old song many children still sing: Be careful little eyes what you see and little ears what you hear. Thanks to Bob and his latest contribution, when it comes to media and music consumption, that very difficult job has been made easier.

> JIM DALY
> President, Focus on the Family

Don't let technology build a wedge between you and your kids. In order to rise above the challenges that our ever-changing world presents, you need to have a united front at home. *Plugged-In Parenting* is a street-smart, grace-filled approach to preparing your kids to succeed in a media-driven culture.

> DR. TIM KIMMEL
> Author, *Grace-Based Parenting*
> DARCY KIMMEL
> Co-author, *Extreme Grandparenting*

There has never been a more urgent need for children (and their parents!) to exercise discernment when it comes to making choices about media and entertainment. With cutting-edge content and practical steps for implementation, *Plugged-In Parenting* equips the parents so that they may equip their children. This is a resource that I strongly encourage parents to read.

> ALEX MCFARLAND
> Author, *Stand Strong in College*

Plugged-In
Parenting

BOB WALISZEWSKI
DIRECTOR OF
plugged`in.

How to Raise Media-Savvy Kids
with Love, Not War

Tyndale House Publishers, Inc., Carol Stream, Illinois

Plugged-In Parenting

Copyright © 2011 Focus on the Family

A Focus on the Family book published by Tyndale House Publishers, Carol Stream, Illinois 60188

Focus on the Family and the accompanying logo and design are federally registered trademarks of Focus on the Family, Colorado Springs, CO 80995.

TYNDALE is a registered trademark of Tyndale House Publishers, Inc. Tyndale's quill logo is a trademark of Tyndale House Publishers, Inc.

Cover design: Jennifer Ghionzoli
Cover photograph of family copyright © CSA Plastok/CSA Images/Getty Images. All rights reserved. #71533912 Cover photograph of cord taken by Dan Farrell. Copyright © by Tyndale House Publishers, Inc. All rights reserved.

Library of Congress Cataloging-in-Publication Data
Waliszewski, Bob.
  Plugged-in parenting : how to raise media-savvy kids with love, not war / by Bob Waliszewski.
    p. cm. — (Focus on the family)
  Includes bibliographical references and index.
  ISBN 978-1-58997-624-5 (alk. paper) *4723 1203 12/11*
  1. Mass media and children. 2. Parenting. I. Title.
  HQ784.M3W34 2011
  302.23—dc22
                        2010048751

Printed in the United States of America
1 2 3 4 5 6 7 / 16 15 14 13 12 11

This book is affectionately dedicated to my best friend, advisor, counselor, confidant, dedicated companion, and love of my life, Leesa.

You lived (and still do) these principles way before the Holy Spirit began to instill them in me, and for that I am eternally grateful. Much of what I now know, believe, practice, and teach began by watching you and attempting to model your well-lived life. Even as I've rubbed shoulders with many who've failed, compromised, and cut corners, your wisdom, purity, and Christian maturity have been rock-solid. Would this book have been written if we hadn't met and fallen in love? I don't think so. Iron sharpens iron, and you've honed me over our three-plus decades together. During the seven years I was a Christian before we exchanged vows, I was mostly ignorant of the importance of honoring the Lord with my media choices. You, on the other hand, believed you should honor Him with all your choices. Like so many, I had compartmentalized entertainment and made media decisions my way. Thanks for patiently being an incredible source of inspiration, and a solid example of a Christ-centered woman!

contents

part three
Keeping the Peace and Passing It On

Acknowledgments

As I explain in the fifth chapter, the seeds of this book were planted when a teenager in my youth group handed me a teaching cassette tape, the content of which forever changed my life. Thank you, Todd O'Connell. I would guess that you don't even remember doing it. But I've never forgotten. That tape's primary message not only planted a spiritual seed, but watered and germinated it, too. As I listened, the lightbulb finally went on for me. Yes, I began to see, Jesus does care about my music choices. When I digested that simple truth, it only made sense that He also cared about the rest of my entertainment choices.

Thank you, Leesa, Kelsey, and Trevor, for allowing me to share several of your stories in this book. I think they will resonate with readers who will be able to see themselves in your (our) lives.

Appreciation is also due Alanna Gosey, who helped me cite my sources more accurately. Thanks, too, Alanna, for helping me with some of the research, as did Mauri Mays, a former Plugged In assistant. Thanks, Mauri!

An important interview referenced in this book—that of school shooter Jamie Rouse—would not have happened without the help of media specialist Phil Chalmers. Thanks, Phil!

John Duckworth, many thanks are due you, my editor, as you pored over my rough manuscript and smoothed out the many ragged edges. You helped create order, flow, and continuity—without interrupting my style, my passion, or my verbiage. How'd you do that? This ability is both a gifting and a calling!

Certainly I'd be amiss if I failed to acknowledge the entire Plugged In team. Throughout this book there are bits and pieces from each of you—a quote, a stat, a news article. Perhaps even one or two of the principles I highlight in this book came, at least in part, through a conversation we had driving to Denver for a movie screening or as we shared in one of our "Show 'n' Tell" meetings. It's hard to recall how everything came together, but I know we share a like passion—and over the years, I became a better writer, researcher, and "teacher" because I've rubbed shoulders with you, my colleagues.

When it comes to others at Focus on the Family, quite frankly there are far too many to mention here. Many who weren't part of this book directly have affected it indirectly. Those who've helped me share this message on the radio, the Web, TV, and through other outlets have been part of these pages. Thank you all. But special thanks are due to Jim Daly, Clark Miller, Leon Wirth, Yvette Maher, Jan Shober, John Fuller, Bob Dubberley, Jay Barwell, Trent Chase, Dr. Bill Maier, and H. B. London. Not only do you believe in me, but each of you has allowed me to have a significant voice at Focus—and to many people around the world.

Thank you, Dr. James Dobson, for allowing me to share about the great need for media discernment in your book *Bringing Up Girls*. The opportunity to provide an entire chapter gave me greater confidence that an entire book on the subject could someday prove to be a blessing to families of faith.

Finally, and most importantly, I want to thank the God of the universe—Father, Son, and Holy Spirit—for rescuing me out of darkness into light at the age of 15. Then, despite my many mistakes and shortcomings, You allowed me to share in this wonderful, wonderful calling of setting captives free—captives enslaved by what they consume and by the false philosophies of this world. Thank You, my God, my Friend, my Creator! You truly do use the foolish to address the wise.

part one

Deciding Where You Stand as a Parent

one

Is This Stress Necessary?

My cell phone began its vibrating "ring," but this was an important meeting. I let the call go to voice mail. When I listened to the message shortly afterward, the caller was insistent: "Bob, call me back as soon as possible." It was a man I'll call John (not his real name).

I dialed his mobile number. "What's up, John?"

He explained that as he'd walked through his living room the previous evening, he'd noticed his 15-year-old daughter watching a Disney Channel program he didn't know much about. But it made him uncomfortable. He angrily ordered her to turn off the television, saying, "I just don't like the boy-girl thing" on that show.

His daughter promptly burst into tears and grudgingly turned off the TV.

But that was just the beginning. Soon the incident escalated into the family version of World War III.

John's wife, disagreeing with his decision, heatedly and in no uncertain terms expressed how she felt. A fight ensued, with both spouses insisting they were handling the situation appropriately. But before heading off to bed irritated, the couple agreed on one thing: John would call me in the morning and ask my opinion about the whole matter. Both would abide by my decision.

I would be the tiebreaker. No pressure!

I'll tell you where I came down later in this book. At this point, I just want to assure you that family entertainment-related battles are common—although most parents don't call me to arbitrate them.

You know the kind of clash I mean. Perhaps it's arguing over how much time your preteen or teen spends on social networking sites like Facebook or Twitter. Maybe it's your daughter's decision to watch that horror film at last weekend's slumber party even though she'd promised to call if that temptation ever arose. Or it could be borrowing your 16-year-old son's car, turning on the ignition, and getting blasted with profanities from the CD he left in the stereo, a disc you had no idea he even owned.

So here's the question: Since disagreements over what to watch, play, text, listen to, click on, download, and read cause so much conflict, is all the stress worth it? Why not just adopt a "Don't ask, don't tell" policy when it comes to your family's media diet?

To Tell the Truth

At this point you may be thinking, *I know where this is going. This guy has an ax to grind. He wants to make the media look as bad as possible. That's how he makes a living. How can I trust him?*

I understand. I've faced that challenge before.

Trust was an issue recently when my wife Leesa and I were looking for a used car with decent gas mileage. Turning to Craigslist, we found one. As I read the online listing, I was determined that if the vehicle was as advertised, I wanted it. When I called, a young man answered and explained that he was helping his mother sell her car. What I didn't know was that the mother and son had emigrated from China just four years before. The teenage son had picked up English rather quickly, but his mother had not.

"Well, would you take a personal check?" I asked.

"No," was the response.

"Well, we're coming up anyway and we'll figure it out later," I said. At Leesa's suggestion I ran to our bank and withdrew the cash.

Arriving several hours later to inspect the vehicle, we saw it had been represented accurately. "Yes, we want it," I declared, "and I have the cash to seal the deal."

The young man said I'd need to talk to his mother at work. Going to her place of employment, I told her I wanted to buy the car. Despite the language barrier, she clearly understood. But when I pulled the wad of cash from my pocket and explained how we would be paying for it that very day, the deal suddenly was in jeopardy.

"Could be . . . counterfeit," she blurted.

Standing there with more cash in my pocket than I'd ever carried before, all in $100 bills, I had a major dilemma: How could I convince this lady that I wasn't trying to cheat her, that the money was genuine? I tried assuring her the bills were real, that I'd just gone to the bank. I smiled politely and tried to look like an honest man (a challenge in itself). Nothing seemed to work.

In broken English she explained that in China it was very common for people to cheat others using counterfeit currency. As a relatively new person in the United States, she was determined not to get swindled.

I can't blame her. Fortunately, Leesa soon joined me after doing some shopping. Instantly the Chinese lady trusted her—not me—and said she would accept our cash and sign the paperwork!

I tell that story because in this book I'm doing my best to offer what's real, genuine, and true. But I'm afraid some readers won't buy it, believing what I'm offering is counterfeit.

Maybe you, like the Chinese lady, have had experiences that make it hard to trust anyone who comes bearing a pocketful of $100 bills—or arguments and warnings and advice about how the media might affect your kids. Perhaps you've made some assumptions about whether your family's media diet really matters, and whether it's worth the stress of making that diet a healthier one. Maybe you've even been believing a myth or two or three.

Since I can't bring my wife along to convince you, may I ask that you read this book with an open mind? I'll try to earn your trust. My message may not always be pleasant—but it's the real thing.

The Waliszewski Experience

Speaking of honesty, I have to say the following in the interest of full disclosure: As our children grew up, my wife and I seldom battled with them over entertainment decisions. I'm thankful for that, but realize I run the risk of alienating and discouraging you if your experience is different. You might feel our family somehow lived above the fray—something you believe is totally unrealistic for you. I hope you won't see it that way; instead, I hope you'll take heart that although entertainment can be a battleground, it doesn't have to be a bloody one.

I believe the major reason my wife and I didn't regularly bicker with our children over media decisions was our effort to follow the principles I'll share in this book. But we weren't exempt, either.

For instance, when our daughter Kelsey was in middle school, a certain R rated film came out that was *the* talk of her classmates—and the rest of the nation. As R rated films go, it was on the lighter side, but still contained enough objectionable content that we just weren't comfortable letting her see it. According to our daughter, "all" of her friends had viewed this particular movie (which of course wasn't true, but many had). She was convinced she should see it, too.

If you've dealt with a similar situation, you can imagine how Kelsey felt—that her status as a maturing young adult was on the line. She certainly didn't want a reputation for being the girl who was only allowed to watch *Cinderella,* TV Land reruns, and movies filmed in the 1940s and '50s.

I'd love to say this challenge had a happy ending at the time. But it didn't. Even though many, many Christian parents were allowing their kids to see this one, we believed we were making the right decision by putting our foot down. There was no compromise that would make her happy and allow us to stay true to our values. The answer was no. End of story.

Well, not quite. Kelsey is in her early twenties now; recently my wife and I talked with her about her growing-up years. I asked her to describe the most difficult "media moment" in her upbringing. She recalled the situation I've just described. Then I asked, "Knowing what you know now, what would you change if you had to live this time all over again?"

"Not a thing," she replied. Chuckling, she recalled how badly she'd wanted us to let her see that film. But she's glad now that we drew a line in the sand and didn't waver. Whew! It took almost a decade to discover that even from our daughter's perspective we made the right decision.

Setting healthy entertainment boundaries in your home may mean you won't see much buy-in from your kids—at least in the present. But stay the course. Don't waver. A better time probably is coming.

Why is this important? Because navigating today's entertainment successfully is a big deal even though we live in a culture that says it's not. For millions, media decisions are made as casually as buying a gallon of milk or a loaf of bread. I can't tell you the number of deeply troubling R and PG-13 movie screenings I've attended that included parents with young children—even toddlers and those around four or five! Sadly, these parents don't have the gumption to walk out and take their children with them when things decline from risqué to soft porn or from violent to gruesome. I can't even imagine the battles these children will face with issues like sexuality as they grow older.

Chances are you already know, deep down, that helping your kids make wise entertainment choices is important. But it's easy for many of us to avoid taking action. That's because we've latched on to some convenient untruths that seem to excuse us from tackling our responsibilities as parents.

Media Myths that Matter

As ridiculous as it now seems, there was a time I believed I could beat Billie Jean King in a game of tennis if given the opportunity. This wacky thought occurred to me during the much publicized 1973 match between King and Bobby Riggs.

That wasn't the first time I'd made a questionable assumption. After being exposed to Greek mythology in kindergarten, I became convinced that human beings could fly if given the right amount of feathers (never mind that I'd never seen anyone do that). I also believed that if I read a book by candlelight, I would eventually lose my vision.

All of us can point to things we once believed that we now know are totally false. I'm glad that many years ago I accepted the fact that

I'll never be able to fly. Nor do I stand even the slightest chance of returning the serve of Billie Jean King—even in her later years—much less coming out victorious in a match. And I've read many things by low light; my eyesight isn't what it used to be, but I can't blame the lack of lumens.

Living successfully involves the ongoing process of sorting out fact from fiction. There are several myths about the impact of entertainment, the nature of biblical discernment, and the parent's role. Some sound quite appealing. A few may appear to work. Others may look spiritual on the surface. But believing them can have unintended consequences. I'd like to highlight seven of them.

Myth #1: "It's No Big Deal"

Focus on the Family received a letter from Larry, a Michigan father, who accompanied his correspondence with 13 CDs. All but one were stickered with Parental Advisory warnings. Among other things, Larry wrote this: "My son is hooked on degrading, offensive music. After 14 years of Christian schooling, church, and Sunday school, he is rejecting Jesus and Christianity—please get the word out [before] more children fall for this God-insulting music."

Ask Larry if it's true that a child's media diet is no big deal. I guarantee he'll eloquently make his case to the contrary. For him, and many parents like him, this myth was shattered by personal experience and heartache.

Can the choices Larry's son made regarding music be blamed for his abandoning the faith? Yes and no. Music is a powerful influence. But there may have been other factors, too—like peer pressure, his relationship with his parents, a traumatic loss, a lack of real friends, bullying, poor self-image, experimentation with drugs or the occult, a sexual relationship, or false theology. But I agree with Larry that, at the minimum, his son's media choices played not only *a* role, but a *significant* role.

Maybe your child is not battling the same issues as Larry's son. But the chances are great that your young person's faith has been marred somewhat by what he or she listens to, watches, or plays—if those media choices lean toward the unsavory side.

If you do have a child like Larry's in your home, you know that any attempt to "meddle" can get messy. You've heard the advice that we should pick our battles carefully—and we should. Is this one to skip?

I don't think so. Not only should we stand our ground; we need to come fully armored and prepared for the long haul. Entertainment really is a big deal—especially when it has immediate consequences and eternal ramifications.

Myth #2: "Just Get 'Em Saved"

Many parents—though they wouldn't state it quite this way—believe that if they can just bring their young person to Christ, good media choices will naturally follow.

It's true that some spiritual conversions include new convictions about objectionable entertainment. But frequently this isn't the case. When most kids accept Jesus as Savior, it's their first step in a lifetime of maturing spiritually. It's not a magic, protective dynamic. Nor does the salvation experience impart a new understanding of media, any more than it imparts the ability to windsurf, fly-fish, or snow ski.

In fact, it may come as a surprise that evangelical teens seem to consume media much as their non-Christian peers do—at least according to a limited number of studies. One such study appeared in *The Barna Report 1992-1993*, making the disturbing discovery that "Christian young adults are more likely than others to have watched MTV in the past week" (42% compared to 33% respectively).[1] More recently, a February 2011 online survey of 240 ethnically diverse 10- to 15-year-olds—admittedly a small sampling—found that evangelical tweens were more likely to have viewed an R rated movie in the past three months than their non-evangelical peers were (35% compared to 26% respectively). This survey also found that one of every four evangelical tweens watched MTV's *Jersey Shore*, 38 percent said they watch the sexually obsessed *Two and a Half Men*, and 35 percent viewed *Glee*—roughly the same percentage as non-Christian tweens.[2]

At best, beginning a relationship with God helps the new believer want to please Him more deeply. That can bring a new openness to honoring Him with choices that never seemed important before. But it's far from automatic.

Myth #3: "They'll Learn by Osmosis"

Many moms and dads seem to assume there isn't a whole lot to teach about making wise entertainment decisions. They seldom bring the subject up and have never had a pointed conversation about media and its influence.

If asked, they'd admit that they've done little in the way of verbal training. For them, it's all about modeling. They believe that if they practice media discernment themselves, their children will soak in all the right ingredients to make wise entertainment choices.

I can't underscore too many times how important setting a positive example is. But it's simply not enough. Our children also need to *hear* regularly from our own lips how important it is to guard our hearts. They need to understand from us *verbally* what's expected, and why the Lord's heart aches when we disobey and dishonor His commands.

Myth #4: "The Youth Group Can Do It"

A lot of parents feel that if they get their youngster to regularly attend the youth group at their church, that son or daughter will become media savvy. It's true that some youth leaders are quite knowledgeable about media discernment and teach along those lines at youth group meetings. But a number of them don't.

Frankly, some youth leaders simply don't get it when it comes to honoring Christ with their personal entertainment choices. As a result, they don't teach on the subject. I know this firsthand; as a former youth pastor myself, I was halfway through my youth ministry "career" before the Lord got hold of this area of my life.

A rock-solid youth group can make a huge, positive difference in your young person's life. But you can't assume this particular job is getting done. I'd suggest sharing a cup of coffee with your church's youth pastor to find out his convictions on a number of issues—media included.

Myth #5: "I Survived, So My Kids Will, Too"

Plenty of parents can recall making all kinds of poor decisions regarding entertainment during their middle and high school years. Yet somehow they survived the onslaught. These parents put a lot of confidence in their kids' resiliency.

While all that sounds wonderful, there are no guarantees about "bouncing back" in the Bible or in the world around us. Some young people—like Larry's son—turn their backs on God because of the influence of media in their lives. A number of these eventually return, but others tragically don't.

Keep in mind, too, that times have changed since your childhood and adolescence. Much of today's entertainment is darker, more sexually explicit, profane, and gory than what was popular when you were growing up.

Myth #6: "I Have to Wait for an Invitation"

One day a few years ago my family and I had lunch at a local restaurant. Seated nearby was a mother and her teenage sons. I couldn't help but notice that one of the guys had a T-shirt emblazoned with the name of a perverse and violent rock band. When the teens took off, leaving Mom to cover the bill, I went over to her and asked, "Do you mind if I ask you a question?"

She didn't.

"I was wondering how you handle the fact that one of your sons sports the shirt of a band whose lead singer fantasizes on one of his CDs about brutally torturing his mother."

Her jaw dropped. "I had no idea," she replied.

Like this woman, many parents have no idea what's really happening in their teenager's entertainment world. After all, many of our young people have their own television set in their room, don their private earbuds when they're in our vehicles, and head to the movie theater with a simple "See you later."

But for parents committed to passing the "faith baton" to their children—and safeguarding that heritage—having "no idea" when it comes to the world of media is not an option these days.

I'm convinced that some parents *choose* to be uninformed because they fear knowing what's going on would result in a home full of strife. For them, ignorance is bliss. The truth, however, is that it's always better to be informed when it comes to our children—no matter how tempting ignorance can seem.

I suspect the mother I spoke with at the restaurant was more aware than she let on. But I'm certain she asked very few entertainment-related questions of her son that would have helped her get better acquainted with his media world. I'm sure she believed that to open this can of worms would invite at least squabbles and verbal sparring.

In many homes today, the media world is an unfamiliar haunt with a big Keep Out! sign figuratively above the entrance. Parents in these situations are waiting for that sign to come down.

But trust me: Young people rarely remove it of their own accord. It's unrealistic to expect your child to one day approach you with, "So, Mom [or Dad], I really want you to coach me on how I can better serve the Lord in the area of media choices."

So, what's a parent to do if he or she feels unwelcome inside a child's media domain? Start with a heart-to-heart conversation. Your goal initially is just to discover what your young person likes and why.

What you find may dumbfound you—not just your child's preferences, but the reasons behind them. Be careful not to overreact. At this point you're on a fact-finding mission. Ask lots of questions, maybe even taking notes. Listen, listen, listen. There will come a time—perhaps later that day, perhaps a week or two down the road—to respond.

Myth #7: "It Would Be Intolerant to Draw the Line"

Many people are under the impression that Jesus' message was, "You live your life the way you want to and I'll live Mine the way I want to." Anything else, they'd argue, is judgmental and intolerant, or at least condescending.

This isn't even close to the truth, of course. Though clearly guided by love, Jesus booted the moneychangers from the temple, regularly "flamed" religious leaders for hypocrisy, and told a forgiven adulterer to "Go now and leave your life of sin" (John 8:11). Later, the apostle Paul commanded the church of Corinth to expel an immoral brother from fellowship (1 Corinthians 5:1-5), adding, "Are you not to judge those inside [the church]?" (1 Corinthians 5:12).

Despite popular opinion, there's a good and healthy form of intolerance. We shouldn't ignore sinful behavior in our own lives nor in those of our children. Any media pressure that nudges us to act or think in a corrupt way should be rejected. This isn't narrow thinking, legalism, or having a judgmental attitude. It reflects the thoughts and desires of a holy God.

Even the most vile-hearted recognize that there are forms of "entertainment" that are out of bounds. For some, it might have to be something as extreme as a rape scene in a movie, a real murder being shown on the Internet, or child pornography. The real question for most people is not, "Are some things wrong?" but rather *where* one should draw the line.

There is a type of judgment that does displease our Creator—that of condemning another human being. But to evaluate and examine human behavior and spiritual fruit is actually encouraged, even commanded.

Raise Your Kids, Not Your Blood Pressure

Abandoning myths can be upsetting. Trying to get your child to think through his or her assumptions about entertainment and technology can be frustrating—kind of like getting a cat to play the piano. Setting family media standards can ruffle more than a few feathers.

More than ever, though, families need to "learn to discern." Not because there's a shortage of rules, but because some types of entertainment can do real spiritual harm. Abandoning myths, thinking through assumptions, and setting standards are all part of responsible, loving parenting. Does that mean all the stress—the arguments, the slammed doors, the pouting, the "I can hardly wait to move out of here" statements—is necessary?

No.

I can't make the process of teaching your child media discernment a total breeze. But there are ways to make it a lot less painful. You can even find it bringing your family together, helping you to grow spiritually, manage your time, and discover new ways to have fun and communicate your love for each other.

It begins with addressing one more myth—one your child may believe. That's what the next chapter is about. The more you know about answering this objection, the less stressful your parenting will be.

Quotes to Note

"The same violence and gun activity I'm [now] attempting to stop, I once was a part of and played a huge part in promoting. I carried guns and slung dope as a 13-year-old. That's why I feel I owe you an apology."[3]

—Rapper T.I., whose real name is Clifford Harris, speaking at a New York City rally condemning gun violence. The prominent rapper began serving his one-year sentence for federal weapons violations shortly after that speaking engagement.

"He was dangerous to the government. If he had said, 'Bomb the White House tomorrow,' there would have been 10,000 people who would have done it."[4]

—Sean Lennon, son of slain Beatle John Lennon, talking about the influence his rock-star father had on fans

"If my sons told me they wanted to be in the entertainment business, I'd lock them in their rooms until they turned 30."[5]

—Britney Spears

"We're at a time when a chance to become famous in this country can seem like one more inalienable right, as basic as life, liberty, and the pursuit of happiness. But beware, in a culture that seems to celebrate celebrity for its own sake, it can be easy to confuse fame with genuine achievement, or worse, to think of everything short of fame as failure, especially in such an intense media climate. We need to remind ourselves and teach the children that the value of leading a good and decent life away from the spotlight is a real achievement."[6]

—CBS news anchor Dan Rather

"We need to set limits and expectations. We need to replace that video game with a book and make sure that homework gets done. We need to say to our daughters, 'Don't ever let images on TV tell you what you are worth, because I expect you to dream without limit and reach for your goals.' We need to tell our sons, 'Those songs on the radio may glorify violence, but in our house, we find glory in achievement, self-respect, and hard work.' We need to realize that we are our children's first and best teachers."[7]

—President Barack Obama

"I knew my mother loved me, but she never expressed it, so I learned about love from the movies."[8]

—*Playboy* founder Hugh Hefner

". . . Life is much too precious to waste so much of it on TV. When it comes to defending childhood innocence, we have inexplicably invited the principal enemy and potential destroyer into our own living rooms. By the age of six, the average American child has spent more hours watching the tube than he will spend speaking to his father in his lifetime. This is madness and, in a very real sense, child abuse. And the old excuse, 'My kids only watch the quality programs,' does not carry any weight at all. The underlying problem with television and kids isn't quality. It is quantity."[9]

—Film critic and radio talk show host Michael Medved

"Anyone who thinks the media has nothing to do with [the Columbine school shooting] is an idiot."[10]

—CBS president Leslie Moonves

"We better be careful what we are singing and we better be careful how it is presented because we can ruin a nation or change one with the kind of music we allow to be presented."[11]

—Singer Gladys Knight

"Only a third of Americans can name the three branches of government. That's scary. But 75 percent of kids can tell you *American Idol* judges."[12]

—Former Supreme Court justice Sandra Day O'Connor,
promoting her civics-oriented Web site
on *Good Morning America*

"The Internet is very much the Wild West. You wouldn't have sent Laura Ingalls Wilder out in the middle of the night to fetch water from the river. Something terrible could have happened to her. It's the same with your kid. Don't just let them go out there and think everything will take care of itself and [that] your kid is smarter than a scammer. Odds are . . . they are not. And the outcome could be absolutely devastating."[13]

—Kelly Land, a mother from Asheville,
North Carolina

"In today's world, we look at our presidents, our prime ministers, our princes and our potentates and we describe them as our leaders, but they're not. They're merely our rulers. The leaders are the people who change the minds and stimulate the imaginations of the public, whether children or adults. That means the movie makers, the people who make TV shows, the entertainment people in the business."[14]

—C. S. Lewis stepson Douglas Gresham

"Movies are the highest popular art of our times, and art has the ability to change lives."[15]

—Author Stephen King

"Quite honestly, I was very surprised when I read the Audioslave review, and I went on to read maybe a dozen more. I was expecting it to be these kind of fire-and-brimstone condemnations of all things rock and rap. Instead I found the reviews much more thoughtful that the typical rock magazine review."[16]

—former Rage Against the Machine/Audioslave guitarist Tom Morello, describing his introduction to Plugged In's CD reviews

"You must now relate your new life to your recreations. Or, rather, you must relate your recreations to the new life. For recreation must not be the center and the new life fitted into it. If you try that, the new life will die. You must now go over your recreations and see whether they contribute to or dim the new life. They should stay only as they minister to your total fitness. Some recreations do not re-create—they exhaust one. They leave one morally and spiritually flabby and unfit. . . . I find after seeing some films that I have been inspired and lifted. But often a film leaves one with the sense of having been inwardly ravished. . . . You come out drooping. One should never expose himself to such a film—not if he values the higher values. It is like turning pigs into your parlor."[17]

—Missionary to India E. Stanley Jones (surprisingly, written back in 1936)

two

Answering Your Child's Objections

Recently I volunteered to coach a running program for a local elementary school. When our first cross-country meet came around, I found myself driving two team members—one third grader and one fifth grader—to the site.

We'd only gone a few miles when the conversation turned to rapper Eminem. It was obvious both boys looked up to this profane musician. I expressed a differing opinion.

Soon we drove past a building one of the boys recognized. "This is my church!" he exclaimed. For a few minutes talk centered around church attendance, a topic I liked. But just as quickly the conversation switched to movies. The older boy described a scene from an R rated horror movie. He didn't mention the title, but I knew the film instantly—having seen it as part of my work with Plugged In. To describe the film as excessively violent would understate the degree of gore. And language? Try 25 f-bombs and nearly that many s-words, among other things.

Sitting in that car with two boys barely old enough to tie their own shoes, I realized they'd already been exposed to images, language, and occult themes that even adults shouldn't experience. In a very real sense, those boys were victims of what I consider a form of child abuse. Some of their childhood innocence had already been lost.

I tried to say something constructive to them, but I'm not sure my words made an impact.

I wondered about the rest of the story. Had both boys seen the entire film? Had they walked into the room when their parents were viewing it? Had they watched it on cable TV when their parents weren't home? From the conversation it was clear they'd seen too much. It also sounded like they'd had multiple exposures to this type of dark entertainment.

How could this contact not leave an indelible mark on their minds, spirits, and behaviors? I couldn't help but be saddened—not only for these two, but for the thousands of kids who've been similarly exposed.

"But it doesn't influence me!" these two boys might be tempted to say. They'd hardly be alone.

If you've heard your child say those words, you probably were in the middle of an argument over whether he or she could watch a certain movie or TV show, listen to a particular song, or hang around a specific Web site.

If you *haven't* heard those words, you might get your hearing checked.

In this chapter we'll look at what may be the younger generation's most common response to the word "no." The examples and reasoning you'll find here will help you make a response of your own.

Under the Influence

I've heard the following six stories firsthand. Only the names are changed.

- When Judy's 14-year-old daughter Katie was invited by a friend from church to be part of a sleepover, Mom didn't hesitate to say yes. After all, Judy knew the girl. Judy and her husband knew the family. And all the girls involved were from their congregation. What could possibly go wrong?

  Well, as Judy told me: "The girls watched horror flicks; and not wanting to be an outcast, she sat through [one] and had nightmares for months afterward. For my daughter the film was essentially a spiritual attack."

- Paula's four-year-old daughter was always sweet and sensitive. One day, though, the little girl completely stunned her mother by angrily calling Paula the b-word. It didn't take a psychology degree to realize where that seemingly out-of-the-blue vulgarity had come from: The child had walked through the living room the week before, when movie dialogue included the same crudity.
- One father explained how his five-year-old began misusing God's name after getting an earful from an "innocent" Disney animated feature.
- Another G rated release had a family's kindergartener acting like a "hormonal teenager"—not uncommon, since even youngsters unaware of their own sexuality may start dressing and talking in sexual ways as they receive cues from entertainment, dolls, or toys.
- A woman described to me how a scene in a motion picture led her to start cutting herself as an adult, and further escalated her deep depression.
- A friend told me that his driving became dangerously erratic—swerving in and out of traffic—immediately after viewing similar antics in a film. "It was almost as if I had transported myself into the character on the big screen and was driving like I was at Talladega," he said.

All these stories cast doubt on the media-can't-influence-me myth. Telling them to your child won't necessarily change his or her mind, though. We humans love our fiction, and tend to label it as fact when it makes us comfortable.

Three Ways to Look at It

When it comes to media's influence, there are three viewpoints. Your child probably holds one of them—or will soon.

First, there are a few rare individuals who claim that media cannot in any way influence behavior, attitudes, or values.

Second, there are those who believe entertainment can and does influence, but who reject the idea that it could affect them personally. These people would say media influence is felt primarily by the weak, the young, and the impressionable.

Third, there's the view that entertainment not only can and does influence people, it can and does influence *everyone*. After nearly two decades of studying culture, I believe this one is accurate.

Many people believe the first two myths. But countless real-life situations refute them, as you'll see in this chapter.

So why is the truth so hard for so many to accept? Because if they admit entertainment might sway their thoughts and decisions, it logically follows that they must guard how they consume media and carefully choose what they watch and listen to.

And they don't want to do that.

Here's my view: *None of us—including me—is above being negatively influenced by the entertainment we consume.* If we believe we are, we're much more likely to ingest the types of entertainment that can trip us up. Those of us who are followers of Christ may wish our faith magically inoculated us against media influence. It doesn't. Certainly it can help, but it's not a cure-all.

That's why it's so important to challenge our kids when they say, "But it doesn't influence me." The challenge doesn't have to be a confrontation; a calm presentation of the facts will do, and there's no need to present all the facts at once. You're not arguing a landmark case before the Supreme Court, you're encouraging your child to consider wisdom.

So when teachable moments present themselves—when a sleazy beer commercial or a vengeful "love" song oozes from the car radio, for instance—take the opportunity to counter the myth. Here are nine points you could make over the long term, keeping in mind the maturity and attention span of your child. Don't try to use every bit of evidence presented here, and feel free to word it in ways that meet the needs of your family.

Point #1: Advertisers Count on Media Influence

TV programmers have claimed for years that they only reflect society but don't have the power to shape it—which seems odd, considering that they pat themselves on the back when it comes to the power of advertising.

When a Fortune 500 company calls a broadcast or cable channel to talk about buying airtime, TV executives sing a whole different song when it comes to influence. In these sales calls, they explain how profoundly they can affect buying behaviors, rattling on about how a mere 30 seconds of TV time can cause people to clean their bathrooms with a certain spray or pay big bucks to have low-calorie meals overnighted to their homes.

And they're right. They don't flinch when revealing the price tag of their advertising. It was reported, for example, that Fox charged an average of $3 million for 30-second slots in the 2011 Super Bowl, and that 90 percent of these were sold out five months before the event.[1]

But think about it. It's completely irrational for TV execs to argue that their medium can't influence, then go to great lengths to prove that it does. Sadly, very few folks call them on it by pointing out that they can't have it both ways.

An exception is Bill Cosby. Posted near my office computer for a number of years has been this quote from the well-known comedian: "The networks say they don't influence anybody. If that's true, why do they have commercials? Why am I sitting there with Jell-O pudding?"[2] He understands that the media have a powerful influence on society. If a mere 30 seconds can get us to buy pudding, throw back an image-maker soft drink, or post our résumé to a particular Web site, no doubt the same networks' 30-minute sitcoms, 60-minute dramas, and two-hour movies are having an impact as well.

Point #2: Research Shows the Connection

In 2004 the Rand Corporation published a study that linked sexualized television with actual sexual behavior. Among 1,792 adolescents surveyed, those who watched TV programs with a lot of sexual content were twice as likely to engage in intercourse as their peers who watched few such programs. Two years later, the same research group made a similar discovery regarding music: Of 1,461 adolescents surveyed, those who listened to sexualized music were almost twice as likely to engage in intercourse as their peers who listened to very little (within two years after the survey).[3]

Researchers in 2006 at the University of North Carolina at Chapel Hill found that white teens who consume a lot of sexualized music, television, and movies are more than twice as likely to have sex by age 16 as their less-exposed peers.[4] The correlation isn't as strong among African-American teens.

Researchers at Dartmouth Medical School published a report in 2010 finding that middle school students whose parents prohibited R rated movies were less likely to drink alcohol than those who were allowed to watch such films. Almost 25 percent of the young people who had permissive parents had tried drinking without their parents' knowledge, compared with barely 3 percent of those who were "never allowed" to watch restricted films. Dartmouth pediatrician and professor James Sargeant, who co-authored the study, says researchers controlled for parenting style and still found that "the movie effect is over-and-above that effect." Explains Sargeant: "The research to date suggests that keeping kids from R rated movies can help keep them from drinking, smoking and doing a lot of other things that parents don't want them to do."[5]

Other studies again and again point to the same conclusion: Young people *are* affected by what they watch and listen to. In fact, after examining 173 studies involving media and behavior, researchers at the National Institutes of Mental Health, working with Common Sense Media, found that 80 percent of them linked media (defined as television, movies, video games, music, the Internet, and magazines) to adverse outcomes for children—including smoking, drug and alcohol use, obesity, sexual activity, attention problems, and poor grades. Fully 93 percent of the studies found that children exposed to more media have sex earlier.[6]

Point #3: If You Can Have a Positive Influence, You Can Have a Negative One

Yes, entertainment can influence people for the good. I like the way Rev. Michael Catt, senior pastor of Sherwood Baptist Church in

Albany, Georgia, puts it: "Movies are the stained-glass windows of the 21st century, the place to tell the Gospel story to people who may not read a Bible."[7] He should know. His church has produced several films (*Facing the Giants, Fireproof, Flywheel,* and *Courageous*) that have influenced marriages, fatherhood, and spiritual lives around the world. The "stained glass" of *Fireproof* made an impact in more than 55 countries and was translated into a dozen languages. *Facing the Giants* even appeared as in-flight entertainment on a Muslim-owned airline.

Other positive examples include:

- Campus Crusade estimates that the 1979 *Jesus* film, viewed by at least one billion people across the globe, has led nearly 225 million to receive Christ as Savior.[8]

- According to the producers of the movie *Bella*, at least 40 pregnant women who were considering abortion decided to give birth after experiencing the film's strong pro-life message. Other viewers decided to adopt as a result of watching the movie.[9]

- Four-year-old Danielle Suttle sat straight up in bed at 4 A.M. when the smell of smoke awakened her. She ran down the hall to alert her parents of the danger—an action fire officials believe saved the entire family. How did she know what to do? She'd seen Barney, PBS's purple dinosaur, give instructions on how to react. "Barney says if you smell a fire, you gotta get your mommy," Danielle said.[10]

- Grayson Wynne, age 9, got lost in Utah's Ashley National Forest in 2009. Leaning on survival skills he'd learned from the Discovery Channel program *Man vs. Wild,* he was found by rescuers a day after going missing. The program showed him he could leave clues behind to help searchers find his trail—by tearing his yellow rain slicker and tying pieces to trees.[11]

So if entertainment can influence positively, why not negatively? Game show host Pat Sajak put it this way:

Television people have put blinders on and they absolutely refuse—and movie people too—to admit that they can have any influence for ill in our society. And you know the argument. It's, "We only reflect what's going on, we don't perpetuate it." And yet not a week goes by in this town where there's not an award ceremony where they're patting each other on the back saying, you know, "You raised AIDS awareness, there'll be no more child abuse thanks to this fine show you did." The argument is you can only influence for good, you can't influence for ill. That makes no sense at all.[12]

Point #4: People Admit They Were Influenced
Countless people who've done illegal, dangerous, or just plain dumb things testify that they were influenced by media messages. Others might say the perpetrators were using entertainment as an excuse, but isn't there a pattern in reports like the following?

- A number of crimes have been linked to video games in which players are rewarded for stealing cars and committing other illegal acts. Six teens were arraigned in Mineola, New York, following a crime spree that included mugging one man and menacing other motorists with a baseball bat, a crowbar, and a broomstick. The teens, ages 14 to 18, told police they were imitating the popular *Grand Theft Auto* video games.[13]

  In Thailand the entire *Grand Theft Auto* franchise was banned following the murder of a taxi driver by a teen who confessed he was emulating the violent series. The high school senior said, "I needed money to play the game every day. My parents gave me only 100 baht a day, which is not enough."[14]

  Reader's Digest quoted an anonymous, incarcerated gang member from Oakland, California: "We played [*Grand Theft Auto*] by day and lived the game by night." He described how the game became a kind of virtual reality training, and that his gang has been linked to car thefts and at least seven murders.[15]

Even *Wired* contributor Susan Arendt found herself influenced by *Grand Theft Auto*:

I've never bought the argument that a video game's content was likely to influence one's actions, but after several days spent playing *Grand Theft Auto IV* and a recent trip out of town, I'm no longer quite so sure. . . . Despite the reasonable pace being set by the cars around me, I quickly grew impatient with my perceived lack of progress. . . . As I approached a stop light at an empty intersection, the thought flashed through my mind that I should just drive right on through it. I didn't, of course, but the thought was there, just the same. . . . No responsible person is going to double the speed limit simply because he or she spent the afternoon behind the virtual wheel. But what about an irresponsible person? If I, who haven't had so much as a speeding ticket in more than a decade, can feel the undeniable push to do bad things with my car after playing *GTA*, what about someone who isn't so careful?[16]

- Consider Mario Padilla, 17, and his cousin Samuel Ramirez, 16. Padilla was convicted of stabbing his mother to death while Ramirez held her down in a killing they say was motivated by watching the slasher film *Scream*. In a taped confession to police, the teenagers said they killed and robbed Gina Castillo to get money to buy costumes like those used by the killer in the movie. They also told police they intended to wear them when killing several of their classmates.[17]
- An MTV News story in March 2008 noted the increasing popularity of Wicca and witchcraft. "So how does one become a witch?" asked writer Alex Mar. "A surprising number of young witches MTV spoke with . . . said they became curious about their faith through misguiding pop-culture fare like the camp Neve Campbell vehicle *The Craft* and the

Harry Potter series." Mar went on to add, "Guess a few conservative Christian groups were right about that one."[18]

- In February 2011, a 15-year-old Marathon, Florida girl came clean about what had caused the unusual markings on her body. In August of the previous year, she'd told the police she was attacked while out jogging. The truth, it turned out, was even stranger. She and her 19-year-old boyfriend had engaged in "fantasy biting," part of a vampire role-playing scenario inspired by the *Twilight* phenomenon.[19] Similarly, in March 2009, a 13-year-old Des Moines, Iowa, boy was referred to juvenile corrections on assault charges after he allegedly bit 11 students at his middle school. His inspiration? "When police contacted the boy's father," *The Des Moines Register* reported, "he said that his son didn't mean to hurt anyone and that he was biting other students because of the [vampire] movie *Twilight*."[20]

- Nearly every school shooting has a media tie-in of some sort, including that of the school shooter I spoke with personally (see the article at the end of this chapter). In the 1990s, a number of well-documented murders were linked to Oliver Stone's *Natural Born Killers* flick.[21] The next decade saw a few fans of rap artist Eminem confessing to murder, inspired in part by violent lyrics.[22] A list maintained at the Plugged In office—we call it the C&E (Cause and Effect) document—currently includes 308 examples that link entertainment with news events. Not all of these cite specific troubling incidents, but the majority do.

- Many who saw the film *Avatar* said they were strongly influenced by its depiction of the fictional world of Pandora. A site entitled "*Avatar* Forums" received more than 1,000 posts on the topic of how to handle depression after seeing the film. For some moviegoers, Pandora was so beautiful that it made earth-dwelling seem pointless. A fan named Mike wrote on the "Naviblue" site: "Ever since I went to see *Avatar* I have been depressed. Watching the wonderful world of Pandora and all

the Na'vi made me want to be one of them." He added that
his thoughts had turned to suicide; he wondered whether he'd
be rebirthed in a Pandora-like world.[23]

- There are literally hundreds of cases in which media and
  murder are linked. In Walsenburg, Colorado, a teenager was
  arrested for the "thrill" killing of the town's former mayor,
  age 91. An Associated Press story mentioned the 17-year-old
  charged with the crime was "going to kill a friend because
  a song he heard told him to do it."[24] For some reason, the
  alleged murderer changed his mind and went to the elderly
  man's home instead. According to the Walsenburg deputy
  assistant district attorney, the boy was a fan of the gangsta rap
  duo known as the Insane Clown Posse, whose lyrics include
  these:

I collected limbs and made me a zombie
I used so many body parts it was crazy
I killed a whole bunch of [expletive] like what—eighty?
I'm sawing off an elbow.[25]

These are just a few of the incidents that made the local and
national news. I believe that if we're honest, almost all of us have
a story to tell about how we've been influenced by the media. Few
would make the paper or the 5 o'clock news.

Perhaps your story is about a teen trying drag racing after watching a movie about fast cars. Or having a harsh profanity dangle in your
thoughts after hearing it in a song. Or becoming bulimic after seeing
it portrayed as an effective weight loss method on television.

We're all impressionable. When I asked my son, Trevor, if he
could recall a scary movie scene that had bothered him during childhood, he gave me the title of a Christian video! I know fear wasn't the
intended outcome, but that's how it played out in Trevor's mind when
he was a preschooler. That's because entertainment is influential, as
many can—and do—attest.

Point #5: The Memories Linger

Have you ever gotten a tune stuck in your head? All you need to hear are a few bars and it starts involuntarily buzzing around in there. *For hours.*

It could be a commercial jingle or a Top 40 hit. Whether we're humming the last song we heard on the radio before getting out of the car, carrying a hymn from the morning worship service with us long into Sunday afternoon, or trying to clear our brains of an uninvited TV theme song, I think we've all experienced this.

And it's not just the music. The lyrics rattle around in there, too—some of which may be rather disturbing when we stop to think about them.

Sadly, I can recall as a youth pastor humming in my head the lyrics of Eric Clapton's "Cocaine" before stepping to the church's podium to lead worship. I wasn't in danger of snorting any white powder because of these lyrics, but they sure didn't help me usher the congregation into the presence of God, either. Some 25 years later I can still recall this incident because it alarmed me that I could be so easily swayed.

Then there are the visual media. Most of us can call to mind images we wish we could mentally erase—things we've seen in movies, in magazines, on TV. The point is that music and images tend to travel with us. Good or bad, they rarely go in one ear (or eye) and out the other.

Point #6: We Love Endorphins

There's growing evidence that singer B. J. Thomas was right: It's possible to get "hooked on a feeling."

The longer I live, the more convinced I am that music plays a pivotal role in our moods and can create (or at least help create) an emotional state—often a state we want to return to again and again.

Here's an example of how it works with me. After reviewing an objectionable film as part of my work responsibilities, the last thing I want playing in my car stereo system on the way home is something loud and bass-heavy. Typically I'll locate a station that airs praise and worship or listen to a few contemporary Christian favorites via my iPhone. I find these songs refreshing to my spirit.

But I'm also a runner. I wouldn't want praise tunes broadcast over the PA system before a big race. Prior to the starting gun, I want to hear something like the theme from *Rocky* or *Top Gun*. And judging from most of the music I've heard before races, I'm not alone.

I'm also not the only one who believes that music and visual images spark sensations that make a difference. I once spoke with Dr. Richard G. Pellegrino, an M.D. and Ph.D. in neurology and neuroscience, about the effect that music has on our emotions. When I interviewed him he'd been working with the brain for 25 years, and said that nothing he did affects a person's state of mind the way one simple song can.

Having worked in a New York City emergency room, Dr. Pellegrino observed that drug addicts were often more concerned with feelings than with life itself. As overdosing patients struggled for breath, ER staff would work feverishly to prepare injections of Naloxone, a drug that binds the opium high. The result, Pellegrino said, was "sixty to zero instantly." But rather than be excited that their lives were spared, addicts would often come up swinging, upset that the ER team had ruined their high.

What does this have to do with music? Plenty. According to Pellegrino, the same "receptors that bind opium also bind endorphins, a class of natural opioid found in the brain." Experiments have shown that if you give Naloxone to a group of people and ask them to listen to their favorite songs, it suddenly becomes an intellectual exercise— the intensity of the emotions seems to diminish.

So music (and visual media, I believe) has the power to shape our feelings. This isn't bad; after all, God invented music and people to listen to it. The trouble comes when we become addicted to the feelings and choose the wrong music to get them—or when we keep picking songs that put us in an angry, depressed, or rebellious state.

Point #7: Media Make Morality Tougher
After I spoke to one group of teenagers about their need to honor Christ with their entertainment choices, a young man came up to challenge me about a motion picture I'd mentioned. He strongly disagreed

with my opinion that this film was full of problematic content (including two steamy sexual scenes and frontal female nudity). He went on to say that although the flick was relatively new, he'd already seen it five times.

Dismissing my objections, he rambled on about the film's incredible special effects and story line. I didn't disagree with either of those things, but tried to explain that we shouldn't be basing our film viewing solely on those elements. I couldn't seem to convince him.

Finally I asked him, "Have you ever watched this film and after viewing the nudity or sexual scenes found yourself battling with lust and impure thoughts and desires?"

He didn't answer. He just quietly lowered his head and walked away. I have to assume that if his answer to my question was "No," he would have told me. But his silence spoke volumes.

It's a rare film, television program, mainstream album, or Web site that, when referring to physical intimacy, does so in a Christ-honoring fashion. On the contrary, sex outside of marriage is often made to look superior to what God has in mind. For a teen wanting to wait for that future lifelong partner, there won't be much help from Hollywood, the Internet, or the recording industry.

When the media depict sexually involved unmarried couples as the norm, and every form of perversity as either normal or funny, should it surprise us when our kids find it harder than ever to fight sexual temptation? In 2006, the *Journal of Adolescent Health* reported that teens who absorbed sexually explicit entertainment most frequently were up to 2.2 times more likely to have had sexual intercourse by ages 14 to 16 than those who consumed the least. The study noted, "Adolescents who are exposed to more sexual content in their media diets, and who perceive greater support from the media for teen sexual behavior, report more sexual activity and greater intentions to engage in sexual intercourse in the near future. . . . Media may serve as a kind of sexual 'super peer' for adolescents seeking information about sexuality because sexual content in the media is ubiquitous and easily accessible, and sexual messages are delivered by familiar and attractive models."[26]

Kids from Christian families aren't immune to this influence. Take the young man who talked to me after my presentation, for example.

First, he was active in a church youth group—or at the very least chose to attend this particular evening. He'd had some exposure to biblical principles and the concept of living for Christ. But none of that seemed to matter much, at least in this "compartment" of his life.

Second, he was highly immersed in popular culture—as are most kids. He placed a high value on his own enjoyment. If he had to rate its importance, I think he would have given it a solid 10 on a 10-point scale.

Third, he made entertainment choices without considering how they might battle against sexual purity in his own life. He apparently didn't bring his Creator into the decision process. The fact that he'd seen this film five times suggested that his parents weren't highly involved, either. It didn't seem to occur to him to consult God's Word on the subject.

More than three-quarters of teen boys (78 percent) feel there's "way too much pressure from society" to be sexually active, according to a survey conducted by *Seventeen* magazine and the National Campaign to Prevent Teen and Unplanned Pregnancy.[27]

I don't worry that most Christian teens are going to become the next Virginia Tech–like shooter. But with this kind of pressure coming from many movies, songs, TV shows, and Web sites, I do worry about how increasingly tough it is for kids to reserve sexual activity for marriage. As hard as it is for our kids to honor Christ with their sexuality, it becomes exponentially harder when they sabotage themselves by intentionally consuming media with sexual themes and messages that conflict with God's design.

Point #8: Society Recognizes the Impact of Onscreen Smoking

If I could magically snap my fingers and make six destructive behaviors suddenly disappear from the world, smoking probably wouldn't be one of them. For me, there are bigger fish to fry. But it's a good thing that for some reason, people on both sides of the political aisle have come together to try to reduce teenage smoking. They're calling for entertainment companies to stop glamorizing lighting up.

What's more, a lot of research dollars have gone into studying the effects of onscreen smoking and how it may influence young people to begin this harmful habit. Surprise—onscreen smoking actually influences real-life smoking!

A study published in the *Archives of Pediatric and Adolescent Medicine* in 2008 found that white U.S. teenagers who watch a lot of R rated movies are a whopping *seven* times more likely to start smoking than their peers with less exposure to such films. According to Senior Scientific Editor Dr. Ronald Davis, "Depictions of smoking in movies is causally related to youth smoking initiation" with "adolescents with higher exposure to smoking in the movies" 2 to 2.7 times more likely to try smoking.[28]

A few years before the *Archives of Pediatric and Adolescent Medicine* report, another nationwide study of more than 6,500 children and 532 movies revealed that 38 percent of smokers ages 10 to 14 started their habit after seeing it on the big screen. Though no more than 10 percent of all kids in this age group smoke, those who witnessed the most smoking onscreen were 2.5 times more likely to smoke than those who saw the least.[29]

Hollywood screenwriter Joe Eszterhas (*Basic Instinct, Showgirls*) explained in an interview how a Jerry Lee Lewis movie called *High School Confidential* helped influence his own smoking habit. He added, "I began running across other people in normal day-to-day life who also recounted specific moments and specific actors [that led to their smoking habits]. A man in my local video store remembered Robert Mitchum smoking in a movie and it led him to smoke; I got an email from a man in Japan who remembered Humphrey Bogart and how it led him to smoke; I got another email from a man who remembered the [original] James Bond movies and how they got him smoking."[30]

There's wide agreement that the media have inspired many people to smoke. So why only tackle the issue of smoking? Why not the sexual messages? The language? Drug and alcohol abuse? The violence? If it's true that smoking on the screen is linked with actual smoking, then it logically follows that other onscreen behaviors must be linked to real-life deeds as well.

Point #9: Hollywood Insiders Admit Their Influence

It's one thing for people like me to claim that entertainment often has a powerful, negative effect. But when the folks who produce that entertainment say the same thing, isn't it time to pay attention?

For example, after wondering whether the 2007 Virginia Tech shooter was influenced by the violent Korean film *Oldboy*, screenwriter Mike White (*School of Rock*) wrote this:

> The notion that "movies don't kill people, lunatics kill people" is liberating to us screenwriters because it permits us to give life to our most demented fantasies and put them up on the big screen without any anxious hand-wringing. We all know there's a lot of money to be made trafficking in blood and guts. Young males—the golden demographic movie-makers ceaselessly pursue—eat that gore up. What a relief to be told that how we earn that money may be in poor taste, but it's not irresponsible. The average American teenage boy knows the difference between right and wrong and no twisted, sadistic movie is going to influence him. My own experience as a teenager tells me otherwise. For my friends and me, movies were a big influence on our clothes, our slang, and how we thought about and how we spoke to authority figures, our girlfriends and one another. Movies permeated our fantasy lives and our real lives in subtle and profound ways. . . . We [in the industry] know better than anyone the power films have to capture our imaginations, shape our thinking and inform our choices, for better or for worse.[31]

And here's screenwriter Joe Eszterhas again:

> A cigarette in the hands of a Hollywood star onscreen is a gun aimed at a 12- or 14-year-old. . . . The gun will go off when that kid is an adult. We in Hollywood know the gun will go off, yet we

hide behind a smoke screen of phrases like "creative freedom" and "artistic expression."

Those lofty words are lies designed, at best, to obscure laziness. I know. I have told those lies. The truth is that there are 1,000 better and more original ways to reveal a character's personality. . . . I have been an accomplice to the murders of untold numbers of human beings. I am admitting this only because I have made a deal with God. Spare me, I said, and I will try to stop others from committing the same crimes I did.[32]

Not everyone in Hollywood would agree with statements like these, of course. And those who concur are undoubtedly under great pressure not to speak out. But when they do, they can't be ignored.

Objection Overruled?

Whether it's about smoking, sexual behavior, rebellion, or violence, today's research overwhelmingly comes to the same conclusion: Entertainment can and does influence thoughts and actions.

Your child may or may not be swayed by the points presented in this chapter. If you want to influence him or her as strongly as the media do, remember that these facts, figures, and anecdotes aren't ammunition in a shootout. They're support for a way of thinking and acting that you want to encourage because you love your child.

Let that love guide your conversations about entertainment. Healthy media choices are important, but so is your relationship. The more you nurture that relationship, the more willing your child will be to listen.

What I Learned from
a School Shooter

As far as I know, up until the fall of 2000 I'd never been in the same room with a murderer. But in October of that year, I met with school shooter Jamie Rouse at the South Central Correctional Center just outside Clifton, Tennessee.

After entering this razor wire-protected compound, passing through several heavy metal doors, and having my permission-to-enter stamp scanned, I was led to the prison's infirmary. It was there our meeting would take place.

Jamie, then 22, was uncomfortable making eye contact. Though handcuffed, he posed no threat.

But that hadn't been the case five years before. On November 15, 1995, 17-year-old Jamie walked into Richland School in Lynnville, Tennessee, carrying a .22 caliber rifle at his side. Before being tackled by a teacher, he killed two people—a teacher and a ninth-grade student. A second teacher received a bullet to the head but miraculously survived.

Although Jamie now realizes he was dealing with a number of personal issues during those dark days, when I asked him if his entertainment choices played a role, he explained the media had an enormous impact.

Q: I know you would never say the entertainment made you do it, but you definitely feel that entertainment was at least a factor. Give me more detail.

Jamie: When I first started listening to heavy metal music . . . it had very anti-Jesus lyrics and that's what inspired me to carve an inverted cross [on my forehead]. I just thought it'd be cool and I didn't have the strong support at church, support at home, didn't really have anything in my life, I had a big void. I started experimenting into music and unfortunately it was the wrong type.

Q: How did the music make you feel?

Jamie: It made me feel angry and sometimes just evil, outright evil.

Q: Jamie, your dad said something last night about the two of you watching *Natural Born Killers* together maybe a month, he thought, before November 15th. Did that movie play any role in your thinking during this time?

Jamie: I found *NBK* very entertaining. It made killing seem cool. That's the way I took it.

Q: What advice would you give to kids who wallow in violent entertainment—slasher films, listen to violent music all the time, play violent video games, and find them funny?

Jamie: [Back then] I'd think, "This ain't affecting me, you'd have to be weak-minded to let this stuff affect you." And the whole time it affected me—it helped shape the way I thought. . . . All those songs and the movies that make killing look cool—they don't show in the movies what it does to those people and their families. Sittin' in prison for the rest of their life—it isn't fun.

Slayer and a Slaying

"Our daughter, Elyse Marie [Pahler], then only 15, was stabbed approximately 14 times—none of them fatal—and then strangled with a belt," her father David explained to me.

I was already familiar with many of the details of this July 22, 1995 murder, but I didn't realize Elyse's horrific death was so prolonged. I was aware, however, that David's daughter was lured into a secluded eucalyptus grove near her San Luis Obispo home by three teenage boys—then raped and killed. Perhaps this senseless homicide has had the greatest impact on me personally because I had the opportunity to meet Elyse's parents and more clearly understand their grief.

Since then, I've read lengthy court transcripts, newspaper articles, and just about everything I could get my hands on regarding what happened. And I've concluded this: While murders have been happening since Cain slew Abel, this particular one, I believe, most likely wouldn't have occurred if a certain rock band hadn't made killing seem so rational and exciting—and young females seem so utterly worthless.

Where did these boys get the idea to commit such unconscionable acts? "They followed the [rock] band Slayer and took their cues from the destructive messages of death metal music," answered David. "The lyrics obviously had a profound effect."

Slayer's songs typically carry such titles as "Spill the Blood," "Necrophiliac," and "Kill Again." Consider how these lyrics from "Sex. Murder. Art" on the band's *Divine Intervention* CD could possibly implant homicidal thoughts in some unstable fans:

> You're nothing, an object of animation . . .
> Beaten into submission, raping again and again, shackled,
> my princess . . .
> Bleeding, on your knees, my satisfaction is what I need . . .
> Pleasure in inflicting pain . . .
> God is dead, I am alive.

Although hardly excusing the behavior, this may help to explain where Elyse's killers (Joseph Fiorella, 15; Jacob W. Delashmutt, 16; and Royce E. Cayse, 17) got their cues on what to do and how to do it.

Slayer's influence had manifested itself earlier when this trio decided to form a rock band called Hatred—which spewed its own dark, Slayer-like messages. The three adopted the Slayer lifestyle as well.

Slayer's influence apparently fueled a dark spiritual interest, too—a commitment to serve the devil. After the killing,

Cayse wrote in his journal: "I made the switch last night. [Satan] has taken my soul and replaced it with a new one to carry out his work on the earth. . . . I am now allied with the darkened souls." In a confession to one of the chief investigators, Cayse explained that he and his bandmates selected Elyse simply because she had blonde hair and blue eyes, and was known to be a virgin—qualities they believed were needed "to be a perfect sacrifice to the devil."

The boys were convinced that when they murdered Elyse, the devil would reward them with a "ticket to hell," "power and [success to] . . . go professional," and the ability to "get better at guitar."

three

Doing Your Child a Favor

After listening to some speakers or reading their books, you might get the impression that media discernment is something negative—even cruel—you must do to your children. It's all about limits and warnings and turning things off and saying, "No."

The truth is that making healthy entertainment choices is a positive exercise with positive results. When you teach your kids to consume media wisely, you may restrict them in some ways—but broaden their horizons in others. You help them develop critical thinking skills that can keep them from falling for scams and empty promises. You increase the flow of encouraging messages that build their confidence and steer them away from hopelessness.

Helping kids pump up their "media muscles" is ultimately for their benefit. It's not to keep you from being embarrassed when other parents at church find out what your child listens to. It's not to avoid answering awkward questions about what that couple on the screen was doing in the bedroom. And it's not a chance to play "control freak."

It really is, as the saying goes, "for the children."

Your kids need to know that. They need to hear that they'll gain far more than they'll lose when your family takes a smart, God-honoring approach to screens, songs, and sites. When they understand that, they'll be less likely to react as if you've clamped electronic monitoring bracelets on their ankles.

Media discernment has many rewards; in this chapter we'll look at just four.

Reward #1: Find Time to Explore the Real World

The sheer amount of time kids spend on entertainment and technology is stunning. For instance, the average U.S. teenager sends or receives 2,899 text messages per month (compared to 191 calls), and views 31 movies a year.[1] A 2009 Nielsen report found that the same teen watches three hours and 20 minutes of TV every day.[2]

But that's not all. According to a 2010 Kaiser study of 2,002 kids ages 8-18, when you add up the time spent with all forms of entertainment and technology-related consumption, the typical young person racks up a staggering seven hours and 38 minutes each day—up from six hours and 19 minutes a decade earlier.[3] In other words, the average U.S. child in this age group "works" the equivalent of a full-time job when it comes to movie, DVD, and TV viewing, listening to music, spending time with YouTube or similar online video providers, texting, electronic gaming, surfing the Internet, and social networking.

The problem isn't just *what* kids are watching and listening to. It's also what they're missing while they're watching and listening to so *much*. The same Kaiser study found that the average U.S. child spends 30 hours in school each week and about 15 hours with parents.[4] That means that when it comes to training young people, media clock in at about 40 hours per week; school, 30 hours; parents, 15 hours. Any question about who may be having the greatest impact?

Even kids ages two to five spend 32 hours a week parked in front of the tube, according to another study, while 6- to 11-year-olds watch 28 hours.[5] A whopping two-thirds of children live in homes where the television is *not* turned off for mealtimes.[6] And the Associated Press reports that families who send preschoolers to home-based daycare may have to factor in *another* two hours per day of viewing—an aspect mostly overlooked by researchers.[7]

Concerned observers have been warning for years that our "high-tech, low-touch" society is producing children who can navigate social networking sites and text messaging but don't know how to "interface" in person. Now they're talking about a new malady: nature-deficit disorder. Author Richard Louv makes the case in his book *Last Child in the Woods*:

> One evening when my boys were younger, Matthew, then ten, looked at me from across a restaurant table and said quite seriously, "Dad, how come it was more fun when you were a kid?"
>
> I asked what he meant.
>
> "Well, you're always talking about your woods and tree houses, and how you used to ride that horse down near the swamp."
>
> At first, I thought he was irritated with me. I had, in fact, been telling him what it was like to use string and pieces of liver to catch crawdads in a creek, something I'd be hard-pressed to find a child doing these days. Like many parents, I do tend to romanticize my own childhood—and, I fear, too readily discount my children's experiences of play and adventure. But my son was serious; he felt he had missed out on something important.
>
> He was right. Americans around my age, baby boomers or older, enjoyed a kind of free, natural play that seems, in the era of kid pagers, instant messaging, and Nintendo, like a quaint artifact. . . .
>
> Not that long ago, summer camp was a place where you camped, hiked in the woods, learned about plants and animals, or told firelight stories about ghosts or mountain lions. As likely as not today, "summer camp" is a weight-loss camp, or a computer camp. For a new generation, nature is more abstraction than reality. Increasingly, nature is something to watch, to consume, to wear—to ignore. A recent television ad depicts a four-wheel-drive SUV racing along a breathtakingly beautiful mountain stream—while in the backseat two children watch a movie on a flip-down video screen, oblivious to the landscape and water beyond the windows.[8]

Are your children spending so much time YouTubing, Facebooking, iPodding, and Blu-Raying that they're missing real life? When they see a sunset, do they think it's a gigantic screen saver? Do they prefer anonymous online gamers to the flesh-and-blood kids at church and school?

Helping your family become more media-wise is your chance to broaden your child's horizons. Limiting time spent on the digital domain frees up time to touch, smell, and taste, to run and jump and build and look into each other's eyes. That's the message of authors Stan Campbell and Randy Southern, who address kids directly in their book *Mind over Media*:

> Wasting a few hours here and there may not seem like a big deal. After all, you're *young*. You've got plenty of hours to spare. But each of us has only so much time to make a difference in this world. It's the kind of thing you read about in obituaries:
>
> *Mr. Ponce worked as a school counselor, volunteered at several local homeless shelters, and had seen every episode of* My Mother the Car *at least five times.*
>
> *Ms. Daniels admitted that her biggest regret in life was never having reached the fourth level of* Ultimate Doom.
>
> *Mr. Janikowski is survived by his mother Gladys, his father William, and his 35-inch Sony television.*
>
> Somehow these tributes don't sound right, do they?
>
> You don't have to start writing your obituary just yet. But ask yourself whether the time you devote to the media is time you could be spending on more productive, meaningful things. We're talking about developing interests that drive you, sharpening skills that will benefit you throughout your life.
>
> Think of people who have accomplished remarkable things in the past 50 years or so—people like Michael Jordan, Bill Gates, or your favorite musician. How much time did they spend in Internet chat rooms or in front of the TV? Probably not a lot. Those who excel in any area are the ones who devote their time and energy to studying their craft and making the necessary sacrifices to constantly improve.

After listing achievements kids might choose to pursue—from learning to juggle to designing a Web site for a youth group—the authors offer this advice:

> If you want to see something amazing, choose one of these options (or come up with your own). For three months, devote your "media time" to it. If you usually watch TV two hours a day, try juggling for two hours. If you usually spend an hour and a half playing computer games, try playing the guitar for that long.
>
> At the end of three months, you'll be astounded at the skills you've developed or the relationships you've established. You might even miss your old media friends a lot less than you thought you would.
>
> Psalm 119:37 says, "Turn my eyes away from worthless things; preserve my life according to your word." David didn't know about today's media when he wrote that, but he did see the danger of putting too much emphasis on things that don't really matter.[9]

Will your kids resist if you bring them a similar message? You might be surprised. Chances are they won't be shocked by the news that they could spend their time more constructively. These young people weren't:

> It's very easy to get sucked in. . . . Like [on] a rainy day—you're sitting down, you watch a good movie. And then you're like, "Lemme see what else is on." . . . Before you know it, it'll be 2:00. Before you know it, it's 6:00, and you just wasted your whole day watching TV. The same thing with the Internet.
>
> —*Sholé G.*

> I think you're wasting your life if you just sit on the couch all day and watch movies and TV. . . . I love music . . . I sit in my room and listen to music, but . . . I can't do that all day.
>
> —*Nick S.*

I honestly wish my parents had limited my television use. They sort of [left] it up to me, and I watched a lot when I was a kid. And I definitely should have been reading more and spending more time doing other things, and I regret that.

—*Benjamin C.*

Instead of spending so much time watching TV, read a book. Research some things. . . . Open up a dictionary and open up your vocabulary. . . . Spend time with yourself. Spend time with God.[10]

—*Xica B.*

Give your kids options. Instead of just unplugging the TV and modem and waiting to hear the complaint "I'm bored," introduce them to the children's museum or a backyard garden or the animal shelter. It's true that entertaining them, electronically or otherwise, isn't your responsibility. But especially during the transition from the virtual world to the real one, you'll minimize conflict if you demonstrate that there really are worthwhile pursuits that don't involve pixels, apps, or 3-D glasses.

Reward #2: Less Pain, More Gain

Being a kid these days is no picnic. Pressure to get good grades and scholarships, rejection by more popular peers, crushes on boys or girls who never notice you, drugs and alcohol and eating disorders and terrorism and divorce and the difficulty of finding a job—there are plenty of reasons to be depressed.

So why would a young person listen to music or play video games or watch films that promise to deepen those feelings of hopelessness?

Equipping your child to make wise media choices helps prevent and reverse that downward spiral. It's common sense: Kids who steer clear of "dark" music and occult-oriented or nihilistic games and movies have a better chance of seeing the bright side and bouncing back from the minor and major traumas of the preteen and teen years.

Maybe you're thinking, *My child is in a church youth group. He couldn't be interested in that "dark" stuff.*

I wish that were true. Judging from the "Christian" teens and pre-teens we've spoken with and the letters and e-mails we've received, a substantial number—as with their unchurched peers—feast on a steady diet of hate-filled, angst-ridden songs and images that celebrate activities like strangling a girlfriend, attacking a person with a chainsaw, murdering a baby, committing suicide, smoking crack, and ridiculing Jesus Christ.

But why? I'll let four teenagers respond through the messages they sent us:

> [Dark] music speaks to me. You should realize that the world is not fun and full of life, [but] that the world is full of hate, love, suicide and murder—and we as Christians cannot deny it. You need to look at music with an open mind and understand that not only I, but millions of depressed teens and kids turn to music that understands them.

> [This] happens to be my favorite band. I think that instead of looking at the apparent—cussing, anger, etc.—you should try listening to [this band's] music and messages. . . . They have stopped me from killing myself quite a couple times [sic]. When I listen to their music I can relate to their problems and it helps me get through my life.

> I don't know if you have ever noticed but life can be very messed up for some people. They feel like they have nowhere to go and no one to turn to. That's how [my favorite dark band] has helped many teens around the world. I for one know that they have saved my life.

> I think [the lead singer of this dark band] is a good role model. . . . So how can you say that their music is bad? . . . This [band's] music has really helped me through sometimes

when I was thinking about suicide. Now I go to church and I prayed to God and God did help me. But the music is what made me feel better.

We've all felt the emotions that accompany music. If it's true that we "get hooked on a feeling," it's crucial that the association between music and emotional states is a positive one—one that builds up. If a desirable feeling is paired with music that contains violent, perverse, or nihilistic messages, as your child returns to the music *for the feeling*, he or she also will be bombarded repeatedly with audio land mines.

You may recall how, in my interview with neurologist Dr. Richard G. Pellegrino, he eloquently expressed how powerful a simple song can be. Consider this additional insight from him: "You can pour messages in, and if you pour the *wrong* messages in, they take on a particular power more than the listener understands." What "particular power" was he referring to? The power to build up? Of course not! He was addressing music's power to affect a life in a negative way.

What type of music does your young person listen to when happy? When sad? When angry? When confused? In light of the relationship between emotions, endorphins, mood, learning, and behavior, it's critical that our kids seek out tunes that lift the heart and soul—or are at least lyrically neutral. The style they choose may change from mood to mood, but encourage them to be especially cautious of negative media messages when they're feeling rejected, betrayed, hurt, or lonely.

Keeping in mind the Proverbs 4:23 command to guard our hearts above all things gets a bit more dicey when our emotions are involved. By helping your kids understand that they're even more likely to be swayed by entertainment if their emotions are engaged, you equip them to protect their hearts by rejecting media messages that can damage the spirit.

While other factors can lead a young person to gravitate toward dark entertainment (rebellion, family dysfunction, rejection, peer pressure, a lack of hatred for evil), the mail and e-mails we've received indicate the most common denominator is the "pain factor." No one—teen or adult, Christian or not—wants to suffer, especially alone. For teens feeling that no one cares, a hate-spewing rock CD serves as a catharsis and a means of identifying with someone who appears able to relate. While it doesn't take away the pain, testimonials like the ones I've just quoted say that it serves to relieve the anguish somewhat.

But is there a better answer? If your child is dealing with the pain factor, or might someday, it's important to know.

Many teens dealing with pain can be helped by grasping the fact that rejection, hurt, and distress are negative experiences they share in common with Jesus Himself. The prophet Isaiah tells us (53:3) that Jesus was "despised and rejected by men, a man of sorrows, and familiar with suffering."

Even Christian teens don't necessarily know this. Some think Jesus is an untouchable, cosmic being or force who's aloof and can't be bothered by their problems. The media don't help, often portraying Jesus—in the *South Park* TV series, for example—as effeminate, feeble, or having an anger problem. If your teen "knows" the wrong Jesus, your challenge is to build a bridge to truth. Point out that no one can empathize with suffering more deeply than the One who was whipped, beaten, mocked, spit on, crucified, and became sin for us (2 Corinthians 5:21). He is the One who beckons, "Cast all your cares upon me for I care for you."

For the teen who feels life is not worth living, the revelation that he or she may have the wrong Jesus can be a bridge to spiritual freedom. Instead of aimlessly trudging through life, kids can identify with the Jesus who wants to be their best Friend, who can handle the difficulties they face, and open the door to authentic joy and purpose.

So do the problems vanish? Of course not. But purpose-driven young people gain hope—something lacking in those who live in the deep well of pain. No distraught young person wants to remain in a dark, bleak world. Without someone to point him or her to the Light, sharing the darkness seems the only way to experience some relief.

An angry young woman who knows the pain factor all too well wrote me to protest our stand on destructive lyrics. Her closing words were, "You my friend will rot in hell for that." Rather than take offense, I realized her animosity wasn't really directed at me. She was simply hurting. I wrote back, letting her know that Jesus really cared for her. Her reply was nothing short of remarkable as she explained how she had been abused, and had lost her father and ultimately her faith. Her closing words reflected a significant change of heart, wishing me "the best in your life and faith."

How did she go from hoping I would "rot in hell" to wanting the best for me? It happened when she sensed a glimmer of hope.

This isn't to say, of course, that every young person who's depressed needs only a theological lesson, a happier playlist, or an encouraging note. Don't hesitate to consult a professional counselor immediately if your child shows signs of serious depression or suicidal tendencies.

But in less dire cases, and when prevention is your primary concern, consider the role of media. Bob Steele has; I interviewed him after his teenage son, Bobby, took his own life in 1994 following the suicide of Nirvana's lead singer, Kurt Cobain. I asked Bob, "What would you tell parents today having gone through what you've gone through?"

He replied, "The only thing I can say is to take [entertainment] seriously. Because I didn't. I had no idea that music could influence people to do something like suicide. . . . Kids are curious. They have curious minds and want to know about everything. And if [there] ever comes a day in their life that is very dark and depressing, this music can tell them exactly what they *don't* need to hear."

If your kids have no interest in dark entertainment, count your blessings (and pray for their friends). However, if they're like the ones who wrote us, your first challenge will be to get to the root of their pain. Rejection? Isolation? Fallout from a divorce? Ask the tough questions. Probe. Listen. Teaching media discernment—as important as it is—is a distant second to making sure your teen has a real reason to live (John 10:10).

Reward #3: A Healthy View of Sexuality

What's the point of keeping kids away from sexual innuendo on TV, nudity in movies, and pornography online? It's not to keep them from growing up, but to help them develop a wholesome, biblical view of sexuality and avoid entrapment by sexual addictions.

That's not easy to do these days. When media outlets glamorize certain lifestyles, some young people bite—hook, line, and sinker. One 22-year-old woman explained how TV's *Sex and the City* had influenced her. "When you're [a teenager] you try to emulate people on TV. Carrie smoked so I smoked. Samantha looked at hooking up with random people as no big deal and that's what I did, too."[11] Now realizing that *Sex and the City*'s view is an illusion, that woman regrets her choices. But there's no way to unscramble scrambled eggs.

Similarly, actress Lindsay Lohan confessed that she allowed the tabloid culture to become one of her main sources of information and inspiration. "I would look up to those girls . . . the Britneys and whatever. And I would be like, 'I want to be like that.'" She now acknowledges that it was "really scary and sad." And she "admitted to the things that I've done—to, you know, dabbling in certain things and trying things 'cause I was young and curious and thought it was like, okay 'cause other people were doing it and other people put it in front of me. And I see what happened in my life because of it."[12]

I was reminded how powerfully entertainment can shape sexual thoughts and desires when, in a recent e-mail, J.E. shared his story:

> As a young man I fell into a lifestyle of lust, not justified but easily explained by the shift in culture. I found that to feed my lusts I didn't need to purchase *Penthouse* or *Playboy* or frequent evil places [I believe he meant Internet sites], I only needed to look as far as the nearest movie rental store. Hollywood movies and television became my *Playboy* and *Penthouse*, as I learned that plenty of fuel for the fires of lust can be found in mainstream cinematic films. To forgo a long explanation, God in His infinite grace saved me from this lifestyle of sin. One of the truths which He used to break these chains was the absolute need for me to cut all sources of this fuel out of my life. I found myself at first to be at an impasse. For I desperately wanted to cut this sin out of my life, but in American pop culture I was flooded with the very things I wanted to avoid.

I felt there was no way I could live out Christ's mandate to live in the world and still be not of it. This battle within me would have led to despair had it not been for God's wonderful Word, and the help of your ministry.

I'm glad J.E. is apparently free from this problem. He faced what could have been a lifetime struggle simply because of his entertainment preferences. Notice how he referred to his need to "break these chains." Those who've become addicted to porn, casual sexual relationships, or other compulsive behavior know exactly what he's talking about.

Dealing with sexual addictions usually means engaging the help of a trained counselor. Preventing them usually involves a caring parent, lots of prayer, and a supportive community.

You don't want your child to face a struggle like J.E.'s if you can help it. You want him or her to be a faithful, joyful steward of God's gift of sexuality.

That isn't to say that the battle against this kind of temptation began with the invention of the motion picture, the television set, or vulgar music lyrics. Sexual sins have existed since the fall of man. But moral purity becomes more difficult when our kids battle *themselves* by consuming sexualized entertainment.

Here's how Rev. Douglas Wilson described that self-sabotage in an article we printed in *Plugged In* magazine:

Many Christians are willing to watch, by means of a movie camera, what they wouldn't dream of watching in person. You couldn't get them into a topless bar, and yet they cheerfully go to films where they see far more. Would most Christian men be willing to be peeping Toms, roving the neighborhood? Certainly not. But what if they discovered a woman who knew of their presence and was willing to undress in front of a window? That would be *worse*. What if she was paid to do all this? Worse, worse, and still worse. But what if she is paid lots of money, has a producer and director, does all of this for the movie cameras, and has *millions* of men drooling at her windowsill? . . . [Christian teens] don't want to admit that sexual activity and nudity on the screen is sexually exciting for them. But those who deny that such things affect them are simply deceiving themselves.[13]

Many parents also deceive themselves by denying that their kids could have interest in or access to sexualized entertainment. Poll a group of sixth graders sometime and prepare to be shocked. Researchers in England discovered that 60 percent of boys under 16 have been exposed to pornography, accidentally or deliberately.[14] A U.S. study from the Crimes Against Children Research Center published in 2007 found 42 percent of youth Internet users had been exposed to online pornography in just the past year. Those who deliberately consume porn watch an average of 90 minutes per week. In less than 10 years, the average age at which these boys first encountered porn dropped from age 15 to 11. The research also found that boys exposed to porn are more likely to indulge in casual sex, less likely to view sexual harassment as a problem, and less likely to form successful relationships when they grow older.[15]

Other parents don't seem to think sexualized entertainment is a problem at all. A Lakewood, Colorado, man was sentenced to four years probation and 50 hours community service as part of a plea bargain for "contributing to the delinquency of a minor." His crime? He hired a stripper to entertain his son's friends—at the boy's 12th birthday party.[16]

What if this father had taken the kids to view the same nudity (or worse) at a movie theater? There would have been no outcry, no arrest, no sentencing. Were the boys put at risk solely because the disrobing was live, or is there something inherently wrong with exposing children to lewd behavior? Could it be that many parents are guilty of a form of child abuse when they greenlight problematic films for their kids?

One of the greatest gifts the Lord has given us is intimacy: "For this reason a man will leave his father and mother and be united to his wife, and they will become one flesh" (Genesis 2:24). Jesus added,

"So they are no longer two, but one" (Matthew 9:6). It's that oneness, that closeness, that you want your kids to experience someday within marriage. Helping them guard themselves now from entertainment's counterfeit enticements pays a lifetime of dividends in this area. So does letting them know that's one reason why you're so concerned with what they watch and listen to.

Reward #4: Get Real with God

The Lord has truly opened up some amazing doors for me over the years—one of which has been the invitation to speak to many people about the need to honor God with our media choices. But I've never tried to motivate my listeners to build a fire and burn their CDs, DVDS, video games, satellite dishes, or computer modems. Not that this could never be biblical; after all, some early Christians who'd practiced sorcery brought their occultic scrolls together and burned them publicly (Acts 19:19). It's just that I haven't yet felt a strong leading to encourage the "fire" part.

But I *have* seen how taking such a drastic step has turned out to be a good thing for some Christians. After a colleague and I spoke to one particular group, a young man I'll call J.G. came up afterward to express his strong disagreement with our message. About a year later, he e-mailed to say he'd changed his mind.

> Here's to living proof that Christians spreading God's Word [in this case the message of godly media discernment] can make a difference in someone's life. I have just passed the one-year anniversary of the one event [where you spoke] that has permanently changed my life. . . . [Although initially disagreeing with you, recently I and five friends] one by one tossed our parental advisory CDs and others that were as bad into the [fire burning inside a] barrel. Three hours and $1300 worth of CDs later, six guys had burned the CDs clouding their life. A couple months later I was baptized along with my sister and the fire of God is burning strong in my soul.

This young man had enjoyed a genuine faith, but something was keeping him and his friends from making progress. The spiritual "clouds" were brought on by musical choices that didn't honor Christ. When they destroyed those CDs, they felt free—probably the same way those believers in Acts felt after their scrolls went up in flames!

Some might argue that these teenagers overreacted. I don't think so. For one thing, it took most of a year for the Holy Spirit to get through to them. It was hardly an emotional response to speakers at a conference. It was more like a yearlong wrestling match.

If you're wondering how to keep media training from causing more problems in your home than it would solve, keep J.G. in mind. You might tell his story to your kids. Saying that Jesus cares about what we watch and hear doesn't always go over very well; it didn't with J.G., either, not at first. But he genuinely wanted to live for Christ. In the beginning he wasn't convinced this was a change he needed to make, but the Holy Spirit showed him otherwise over time.

The single most important thing you can do as a parent is to introduce your children to Christ, followed by a concerted effort to help them understand how important it is to please Him. Once they want to do that, setting healthy media boundaries becomes easier. It becomes less an issue of convincing your child to adopt your standards and more a matter of showing that some forms of entertainment displease the Lord and are a huge disappointment to Him.

For young people like J.G. and his friends, pleasing Christ is central to who they are. So if you don't want to fight over entertainment-related issues in your home, pray that your young person would be, like King David, a man (or woman) after God's own heart.

Maybe this sounds unrealistic, expecting far too much of your kids. I'm convinced, though, that one reason entertainment is such a battle-ground in many Christian homes is that some parents believe the most they can hope for is that their young person will survive—not thrive—in their faith commitment. These parents place a very high premium on what I call "sin control." A lot of this has to do with maintaining our image, even in Christian circles. But our children were never called to be mere survivors. They were called to be overcomers, to flourish.

And they can, especially when their relationship with God isn't overshadowed by poor media choices. A truly thriving relationship is a great motivator.

When I was in the seventh grade, my science teacher assigned a 10-page report on microscopic animal life. I liked this teacher a lot and wanted to please her. Instead of doing the minimum amount of work, I compiled 70 pages of material, complete with sketches of protozoa! Why? Because I wanted this teacher to know I cared for her and considered her teaching relevant and important.

I believe the same is true with God. A genuine commitment produces an inward longing to honor the Lord with 70-page volumes when it seems everyone else is getting by with the 10-page minimum. We do this not to earn Brownie points with our Creator, but because His love for us inspires us to greater things.

If you're still not convinced that real-world kids like yours could accept the idea that media discernment offers them spiritual strength, here's an e-mail we received:

> Last year I was listening to all kinds of bad music, even music that
> I didn't particularly like in order to look cool. . . . I felt really guilty,
> like a betrayer, and I knew my relationship with Jesus Christ was
> going downhill. I threw away practically all of my rock tapes and
> began to look into other types of music. . . . My relationship with
> the Lord is growing again and I want to hear everything I can that
> has to do with Jesus.
>
> —*E.H.*

I also like the way my good friend and culture expert Al Menconi stated it in his book *But It Doesn't Affect Me*:

> God's Word doesn't say you'll be a pervert if you watch perver-
> sion. He doesn't say you'll be depressed and angry if you listen
> to depressing and angry music. God doesn't say you will kill
> people if you play first-person shooter games. . . . God's Word
> says if you choose to entertain yourself with empty philosophies

of this world (Colossians 2:8), you will struggle with your faith and joy. How is your faith in Jesus? How is the joy of your salvation?[17]

Do your kids understand why you're so interested in setting limits on their use of entertainment and technology? Do they know these things can weigh them down as they try to run the spiritual race (Hebrews 12:1)? Have they seen in your life the benefits of removing roadblocks from your relationship with God?

As the saying goes, they won't care how much you know until they know how much you care. In words and action, let them know you want to help them clear the decks for a real spiritual adventure—because you and God both love them more than they can ever measure.

The Steak and the Sizzle

Rediscovering the real world, developing a more positive outlook, gaining a healthy view of sexuality, and getting closer to God—those are just four benefits of making wise entertainment choices. There are more where those came from—like learning to think critically, getting more exercise, saving money, and deepening friendships.

Marketing experts advise copywriters to "sell the benefits, not the features" of a product. They also say, "Sell the sizzle, not the steak." In other words, most people don't care much whether an umbrella is 32 inches long or 36 inches long; they want one that keeps the rain off their heads and won't make them look silly when they fold it up and carry it around. In the same way, our kids may need to hear less thundering about a 30-minute daily limit on playing video games and more testifying about the joys of not getting leg cramps from sitting in one position all afternoon.

I'm not suggesting that we take the wrong page from the advertising industry and exaggerate the benefits of media discernment. But if we want fewer fights over choosing family entertainment, it might be worth our while to mention them from time to time.

A Chat with Dr. Ben Carson

Dr. Ben Carson has served as director of pediatric neurosurgery at the Johns Hopkins Children's Center for nearly three decades. He received national attention in 1987 for separating twins joined at the head. Dr. Carson's faith and strong work ethic have inspired him and his wife, Candy, to create the nonprofit Carson Scholarship Fund (for more information, visit carsonscholars.org).

Q: You've expressed concerns about how some media affect learning.

Dr. Carson: Think about the culture we live in. As soon as a baby is able to sit up, we stick him in front of the TV. When they get older and have a little bit of eye-hand coordination and dexterity, we get them a control so they can play computer games . . . zoom, zoom, zoom! That's all they're seeing all the time—fast motion. Then at five or six, we put them in a classroom, and there's a teacher up front who's not turning into something every few seconds. And you expect them to pay attention? It's not going to happen.

Q: Has that contributed to the wave of children being diagnosed with attention deficit disorder?

Dr. Carson: So often, when children come into my clinic they have some kind of neurological problem. But their parents tell me they're also on this drug and that drug for attention deficit disorder. I ask them one question: "Can they play video games?"

They say, "Oh, yeah! For hours and hours, no problem!"

I say, "Then they don't have it. That's pseudo-ADD. What you need to do is wean them off of those things and substitute quality time with you, reading and discussing things."

When they do that, they come back and say, "Dramatic change!"

Q: Your generation didn't grow up with video games, but

television was certainly a big influence. How was it handled in your home?

Dr. Carson: I was an extremely poor student. My brother wasn't doing well, either. My mother didn't know what to do, but she worked cleaning other people's houses and noticed that in the homes of wealthy people, they didn't watch much TV. They spent a lot of time reading. So after praying for wisdom, she said, "I think this is what we'll do in our home!" We could only watch two or three preselected programs, and with all that spare time we had to read books from the Detroit public libraries and submit written book reports.

Q: How did you respond to that?

Dr. Carson: I didn't like it very much at the beginning, but soon I recognized that, even though we were desperately poor, between the covers of those books I could go anyplace. I could be anybody. I could do anything. Using my imagination, I could see myself in a laboratory, conducting experiments. My vision of what my future was going to be changed, and I began to understand that the person who has the most to do with what happens to you is you! It's sort of like taking a baseball player up from the minor leagues who looks out on the mound and sees Roger Clemens. And he says, "Oh, no, Roger Clemens! He's got a 90-mile-per-hour fastball. He's struck out more people than anybody!" Well, with that attitude, you're probably not going to get a hit. Another rookie steps up to the plate—same talent—and says, "Clemens is an old man. I'm going to knock the cover off of this ball." Attitude makes all the difference in terms of the way you face things. And that's what began to change in me as I read. Reading also taught me spelling, grammar, and syntax, which helps not only in writing, but in verbal communication.

Q: [As an African-American], are you concerned about the cultural messages being sent to young African-American men?

Dr. Carson: If you can get the majority of young, black males running around thinking they're gonna be the next

Michael Jordan or a popular rap singer or some fabulously rich gangster, that's really as effective as putting a shackle on their ankle and driving a stake in the ground in terms of long-term success. It really is. That's why my wife and I started our scholarship program and why we created reading rooms that reward young people for discovering books. I was a trouble-maker. I was a negative peer. But once I turned that around and understood how reading could empower me, it changed my whole character.

part two

Making
Rules
Without
Making
Enemies

four

It Starts with the Heart

When it comes to encouraging family media discernment, it hardly ever works to start with rules. If your children don't care what God wants, asking them to adhere to His standards is futile. The best you'll get is outward—and probably resentful—conformity; the worst you'll get is constant conflict. That's why it's so important to begin by understanding where your kids are spiritually.

A few years ago I owned a 1982 Datsun that developed an irritating squeak. I took it in to get it checked—and knew I was in trouble when the mechanic called a few hours later to ask if I was sitting down. His estimate: $802.

In this case, the cost of fixing the vehicle exceeded its value. More to the point, the squeaky noise I assumed would require just a quick adjustment was symptomatic of a need for major restoration.

Our kids emit occasional "squeaks" that indicate a need for spiritual adjustments. If we're sensitive to them, these issues can be handled rather quickly at minimal cost. A word of encouragement, a hug, or a prayer may be all it takes to shift a young person back into high gear. But sometimes these indicators are as foreboding as the dreaded oil light. One of those spiritual gauges involves entertainment.

Time for a Tune-up?

Not long ago I was asked to give a chapel message on honoring Christ with entertainment choices to a group of Christian school students in

Minnesota. Before I arrived, the administration surveyed grades 6-12; among other things, kids were asked for examples of inappropriate entertainment. A high percentage of the students said things that indicated trouble under the hood. Here are a few of the "squeaks" I heard (taken directly from the survey responses):

> "Nothing is totally inappropriate."
> "Undecided."
> "NOTHING."
> "Nothing made for entertainment is too inappropriate. It's all fun."
> "Absolutely nothing."

When kids were asked how to tell if it's okay for a Christian to listen to a song, watch a TV show or movie, or play a video game, their comments included the following:

> "There is no way [to tell]. Anyone can listen to whatever they want."
> "I love all music, from Bach to Slipknot. It doesn't affect you if you don't let it."
> "I watch and listen to whatever appeals to me. . . . My mom doesn't really mind."
> "It's only entertainment. They should be able to decide. Anything's okay."
> "I've become so accustomed to [entertainment that] not much fazes me anymore. But I know it does affect me a lot."

At the risk of sounding harsh, I have to say that these Christian teens need a tune-up. Their value systems are misfiring. You just heard the knocks and pings of this world's hollow and deceptive philosophies (Colossians 2:8).

With my old clunker, I decided the best option was a trade-in. But we can't trade in our children (though there may be days when we'd like to!). We work to fix 'em no matter what it takes and no matter what the expense.

That's especially true when it comes to their spiritual health.

While I'm passionate about helping families become more media-savvy, I do so because of a higher purpose. I believe the most important decision we'll ever make is whether to accept Jesus Christ as our Savior—not whether we live a life free of the media's harmful influences. It's all about loving the One who laid down His life for us. I don't want anything to mar that relationship—and sometimes our media choices do.

If our kids claim a commitment to Christ yet refuse to obey Him, their entertainment diets can serve the same function as an automobile oil light or a temperature gauge. They point to an underlying problem—one that needs attention.

So what can we do as parents? I'd like to encourage you to schedule the following "maintenance":

1. *A spiritual inspection.* Paul writes, "Examine yourselves to see whether you are in the faith; test yourselves" (2 Corinthians 13:5). How can we find out whether our children are living radical, vibrant lives of faith?

We can begin with the aforementioned survey questions posed to the Minnesota students—or the ones at the end of Chapter 7 in this book. Then we can be more direct in asking about their spiritual life and relationship with Jesus:

"How do you feel you're doing spiritually?"

"Do you think you've grown this past year as a Christian? Why or why not?"

"What do you think it would take to move you closer to Christ next year?"

If you hear an entertainment squeak or two, such as "I'm tired of Christian music," "If I don't keep up with that show, I won't have anything to talk to the other kids about," or "Hearing that kind of language won't affect the words I use," probe deeper to find out if you're in for a minor tune-up or a major overhaul.

2. *A spiritual tune-up.* There are many ways to grow and thrive in Christ. Beyond prayer, fellowship, and Bible study, I'm big on two things—summer camp and mission trips. As a father and former youth pastor, I've learned the value of a spiritually strong camping

program. And my wife and I saved up enough money to take our family on a mission trip to South America.

Events like these can breathe new life into your family members' faith. So can attending a Christian music festival together, going to a seminar on apologetics, or taking part in a mentoring program.

Yes, it's a struggle to raise our children to love the Lord with all their hearts, minds, and strength. But I believe we *and* our kids will reap a harvest if we don't give up. Our children can embrace the principles personally, and not just give lip service to ours.

We're in a battle for our kids' hearts and minds. We seem to be outgunned, outmanned, and outspent. But the God who can rout an army with Gideon's 300 and flatten a giant with a boy's slingshot can use our efforts to protect our families and their relationship with God.

If you've been tempted to throw in the towel on this media thing, don't. While there are no guarantees, it's possible to raise children who grasp the concept of discernment—even at an early age. More importantly, it's possible to raise kids who love God passionately—and who develop a concern about their entertainment choices as a result of that passion.

Helping Them Guard Their Hearts

Protecting our kids' relationship with God isn't a one-time event, of course. It takes ongoing effort and reliance on the Lord.

So what has that kind of "maintenance" looked like in our family?

When I started working at Focus on the Family in 1991, our two children were ages four and one. With kids so young, I couldn't help but wonder whether I should be trying to give parenting advice. After all, it's one thing to talk about this when you have toddlers. But I knew some were thinking, "Just wait 'til he has teenagers!"

I'm happy to say that as I write this book, I have a married daughter serving in ministry and a son who's a leader in his college fellowship group. I don't mention this as a backhanded way to boast. I still understand the obvious: Things can change down the road, God has given us all free will, and people do make unwise decisions.

But I also know parents need a reason to be hopeful. And I know from experience that training children spiritually—in the area of media discernment as well as in others—actually can be accomplished.

Early on, my wife and I began to lean on Proverbs 22:6: "Train a child in the way he should go, and when he is old he will not turn from it." We were still well aware that Adam and Eve raised a young man who murdered his brother, and that the prodigal son left a home headed by a caring and loving father. We held on to the biblical principle that our children would be much more *likely* not to take the wrong path if they received rock-solid, biblically based instruction.

We began schooling our children in various life skills—including honoring Christ with entertainment decisions. We were hardly perfect parents, but there were a few things we did that I believe helped our children learn to discern.

First, we resisted the urge to babysit our toddlers with videos. I'm not saying it *never* happened, but it wasn't a habit. When we did let our children watch videos, we used high quality Christian products (*Adventures in Odyssey, VeggieTales,* etc.) almost exclusively. In addition, we paid close attention to the time spent viewing.

Most importantly, we tried to model the concept of making wise entertainment choices and talked a lot about it in everyday conversation *naturally.* What do I mean by "naturally"? While I believe in looking for opportunities to teach media principles, some things in life just make for perfect training times without having to be intentional. Look for them, too.

For example, during a family vacation years ago, the city we were in received two and a half inches of rain. Because our outdoor plans had to be scratched, I decided we'd go see a movie. This was before cell phones could access the Web, so I bought a local paper and scanned the ads for suitable family fare. But I couldn't find a single film that sounded uplifting.

I suppose a lot of people would have looked for the least of the evils and gone anyway. I didn't think that would send the right message to our children—who were scrutinizing me to see what I'd decide! I didn't have to verbalize anything to teach this lesson. My children picked it up clearly because they saw it played out in front of them as we skipped the movies, too.

My wife and I also resisted the urge to be legalistic (e.g., "No secular music in our house!"). We provided positive alternatives to junk, even if they were more expensive.

Finally, we encouraged our children to read about media discernment. As you might imagine, *Plugged In* magazine (then in print; now online) was a frequent visitor to our home when our children were growing up. I watched my children digest the information and principles within its pages, and today the pluggedin.com Web site can serve the same function. I'd suggest finding helpful articles on the site, printing them out, and leaving them lying around. There's just something about entertainment that kids—and the rest of us—find fascinating.

Do You Hate Snakes?

There's another aspect of media discernment that starts in the heart: hating what God hates.

Yes, you read that right. Sure, Christians are called primarily to *love*. But we're also called to follow in the footsteps of Christ, who has "hated wickedness" (Hebrews 1:9). If we imitate His example, despising the very things He died on the cross to save us from, we'll find ourselves steering our families clear of entertainment that glamorizes those things. If your kids don't share that attitude, all the lectures and rules in the world won't make a bit of difference.

Suppose you pull up to the drive-through window of your favorite burger joint. Taped to the order board is a sheet of paper with the following message: "Our shipment of hamburger has been determined by the State Health Department to contain significant amounts of E. coli bacteria. Please order at your own risk."

What do you do? You step on the gas pedal and leave the premises promptly.

Today's entertainment is often "E. coli contaminated" by false philosophies. We need to teach our young people to hate evil in order to help them hit the gas pedal and leave it quickly behind.

Apparently this isn't a universally held viewpoint among parents these days. As I've mentioned before, when I attend film screenings hosted by movie studios or radio stations, the theater is often jammed with an overflow crowd waiting anxiously for a chance at an open seat. As I scan the audience—even for "hard R" rated films—it's quite common to see entire families in attendance, often with infants, toddlers, and elementary-aged children.

What's more, as the film progresses, many scenes that cause my heart to weep inspire the audience to break into rapturous applause or laughter. At times like these I wish more parents would teach their children how to hate what deserves to be despised (not that they should take their children to movies like these with that purpose in mind).

I realize that all this talk of hate could be taken out of context. I understand that among faith, hope, and love, the greatest is love. I realize also that God is love. I get it when the Lord commands us to love our neighbors *and* our enemies. Yes, love is the driving force behind the Gospels, Christ's sacrifice, and our response to God.

But the Bible also commands us to "hate what is evil" (Romans 12:9). And in Proverbs 8:13, we learn that "to fear the Lord is to hate evil."

Sadly, many of us don't really *hate* evil. We tend to tolerate, ignore, live with, and excuse it. Take, for example, reality celebrity and actress (*The Hills*) Heidi Montag. She has talked extensively about her faith, but in a 2009 interview explained how posing for *Playboy* would not violate her spiritual convictions. "I think God created the body. I think we're born naked. We die naked. I don't think it's something to be ashamed of. . . . If I were to do *Playboy*, it would be a huge honor."[1]

It's not my job or intention to judge Heidi's spiritual state. But if we want our kids to have hearts for choosing good over evil, we need to help them understand why we don't just shrug or chuckle at the things God hates. The older they get, the more crucial this becomes; they need to reject evil personally, not just because we tell them to.

Kids (and adults) who don't develop this attitude tend to focus on how far they can stretch the limits, not on pleasing God. In his book, *In the Meantime*, Pastor Rob Brendle explains:

> Cheap grace allows for—even endorses—living close to the
> line because its primary purpose is to get us out of the jam we
> put ourselves in every time we fall into sin. Cheap grace exists
> so we can sin and sin and then be sorry and make it all okay. It
> requires no transformation, just acknowledgment that God loves
> us, wretches though we are, and has provided perma-forgiveness
> through the blood of Jesus. There is no repentance, no turning
> the other way—just sinning and apologizing. . . . We like having
> a license to be weak, to stumble, to fall, and to fail. We like cheap
> grace because it requires little of us beyond some semblance of
> sincerity.[2]

When it comes to entertainment, many people cross the line because of cheap grace, believing it's easier to ask forgiveness than to seek God's view of such "little" matters as movies, music, video games, television, and the Internet. But as Brendle points out, that has a significant downside:

> [Not getting to the root of our sins] leads to living close to the
> line. People who follow Christ this way don't actively resist the
> Enemy, and so they passively aid him. Sin encroaches in our hearts
> like the tide coming in, each wave advancing farther up the beach,
> erasing previous watermarks and leaving once-dry land under
> water. Without active resistance, the devil keeps taking ground.
> We don't usually choose to march on up to the line and defiantly
> camp there; instead, we find that after each successive bout with
> sin, our inhibition has shrunk, our tolerance has grown, and our
> shoreline has eroded just a little bit. And one day we wake up to
> find that we've been living close to the line for some time. With
> a twinge of sadness, we resign ourselves to the reality that the line
> now defines us.[3]

Until we follow Christ's example and despise the things that He died on the cross to save us from, it will be hard—perhaps impossible—to be truly discerning. We can't count on entertainment to depict activities like adultery, gossip, recreational drug use, rebellion, and homosexual relations as anything but glamorous, fun, sexy, and no big deal. What once seemed appalling can quickly seem normal.

Until the early 1990s, for instance, same-sex kissing was taboo on U.S. prime-time television. In 1991 the first lesbian kiss came to the small screen on *L.A. Law,* followed by another in 1993 on *Picket Fences.* But a seismic shift really jolted American culture in 1994, when Roseanne Barr kissed Mariel Hemingway during an episode of the popular sitcom *Roseanne.* When the resulting firestorm of controversy died down, a door had been opened—and has never been shut.

Many have forgotten how quickly the culture went from rejection to acceptance. But those who are pleased with the change remember. Roseanne Barr, 20 years after the launch of her sitcom, explained: "Oh, the lesbian kiss! ABC didn't want to air it, but that was me and Tom [Arnold]'s show. We're like, 'We're doing it!' At the last minute, ABC relented. I knew it was shattering all kinds of middle-class things that should be shattered. To me, it was like a big sociological victory."[4]

Similarly, Michael Jensen, editor of the gay media Web site afterelton.com, made this observation about another ABC television program, *Ugly Betty*:

> What the show does is normalize what should be [in his opinion] a normal thing. [Betty's younger brother] Justin wouldn't have had a big coming-out moment at this moment of life, but it still seems very clear. And the same thing with [Betty's co-worker] Marc. I don't remember him at any point saying, "Yes, I'm gay, I've got a boyfriend" or something like that. It's just completely woven into the fabric of the show in a completely natural way. And I think that's how you get to people. You slip in the side door without making a big deal out of it.[5]

Newsweek's Ramin Setoodeh noted, "A survey by the Gay & Lesbian Alliance Against Defamation found that of the people who say their feelings towards gays and lesbians had become more favorable in the past five years, about one third credited that in part to characters they saw on TV."[6]

The same shifting in cultural values continues on the small screen every week in big and small ways. Author Cole NeSmith in his article "The Dangers of Emotional Pornography" explains how viewing a particular TV show began to chip away at values he held:

> I watched the pilot episode of *Glee* when it premiered a few months before the show was to begin airing regularly. It was decent enough to give some time to the next few episodes. But by the end of episode two, I was getting a little uneasy. As I watched it, I was becoming aware of what the writers wanted me to feel— the good guy teacher to cheat on his evil wife with the gentle co-worker, and the main male character to cheat on his hypocritical Christian girlfriend with his female lead counterpart. It was one thing to want the characters in the show to do this thing or that, but I turned it off in the middle of a scene in which that male student finally decided to cheat on his girlfriend. It wasn't because I was offended at the content before my eyes. Rather, in that moment, there was a transference of energy. I found myself thinking about whose girlfriend I should have stolen in high school and how easy and awesome it would have been.[7]

When we fail to practice "divine hatred," we, too, may find ourselves imagining something evil as "easy and awesome."

When I was a child, my family took a summer vacation to visit my grandparents in Arkansas. To cool off in the stifling heat and humidity, we drove to a nearby stream. There my grandfather led us to a swimming hole, but it wasn't very deep. So we all began building a dam using rocks and tree limbs. When my mother reached for a certain "stick," it swam away. It was a water moccasin, a poisonous snake!

Horrified, Mom rallied us to get out of the water, pronto. My grandfather killed the snake and hung it on a branch to serve as a warning for other potential swimmers.

As with venomous snakes, the proper reaction to poisonous media content is avoidance. But some parents prefer to let their children swim with the water moccasins, believing they won't get bitten. "Well, my kids are thick-skinned," they rationalize. "I know they can handle it." Or, "It may be poisonous, but I know they'll get the antidote next Wednesday night when they go to youth group." Or, "All their friends swim here, and *they're* still alive."

I would suggest that until our children hate poison, they're likely to fall victim to it. That's because despising evil makes it much easier to stay out of snake-infested media streams.

Strike While the Iron Is Hot

So how do we help our kids develop an appropriate hatred for evil? We need to look for opportunities to make what I call *preemptive strikes.*

This may be as simple as saying something provocative like, "I sure hope you grow up to be as good at hating as Jesus is." Then sit back and wait. I guarantee your kids won't ignore that line.

A few weeks or months later, come back to this theme. "Hey, kids, how's the hating coming? Are you getting pretty good at it?" From time to time you also can ask such things as, "Do you think your friends are good at hating evil?" Or, "When does hating evil cross the line to condemning someone, and how can we make sure we haven't crossed that line?" Make sure your kids understand that this is about hating certain attitudes and actions, not about hating people.

You can also use preemptive strikes when consuming entertainment. Let's say you're watching the Super Bowl, and some sleazy beer or body wash commercial begins. Now's not the time to be silent. At the very least, it's time to "talk back to the TV."

Try saying something like, "I really find that type of humor offensive, and I know the Lord does, too." The reason to address a television that can't hear you is, of course, because your children can.

Better yet, ask your children what they thought about what they just saw: "What do you think that advertisement is really selling? What do you think God's opinion of that message is?"

When my children were younger, family car trips were another chance to deliver certain faith lessons. Before getting in the car, I'd mull over a concept I wanted my kids to think about. Mealtimes work well, too. Why not use them to instill media principles by asking your children questions about entertainment?

Another preemptive strike is seeking out couples who've raised children successfully; ask them point-blank what they would (and wouldn't) do if they had to do it all over again. Ask, "What specific things helped your children grasp the concept that Jesus cares about what they watch and listen to? What battles did you face when your children were growing up and how did you handle them?"

Still another preemptive strike is to determine ahead of time that you'll resist the peer pressure to make entertainment compromises based on how other parents handle media in their homes. I'm talking about the tendency to ignore your own biblical values and allow media exposure you're not comfortable with because it seems you're in the minority. Better to ignore what other families are doing (or not doing) and seek the Lord's perspective on behalf of our children.

We aren't called to parent the Smiths' kids (unless your last name happens to be Smith). We're called to parent ours. If we have an opportunity to influence our neighbors, co-workers, or extended family, we should take it. But our primary "mission field" lives under our own roof.

But Does It Work?

"Okay," you may be saying. "It makes sense to influence my child's attitudes instead of just laying down rules. But that takes a lot more time. How do I know it's worth it?"

When my daughter Kelsey was in college, she had several movie-going experiences that revealed the heart she'd developed at home. With her permission, I share three.

In the first case, despite having taken a stand to honor Christ with her entertainment choices, Kelsey compromised and watched an objectionable R rated film with one of her girlfriends. Instead of whetting her appetite for more, though, this breach actually caused the opposite result—personal disappointment that she'd let her guard down. With renewed fervor she decided to stay the course she'd outlined for herself.

The second incident involved watching a PG-13 film. She and her friends made the mistake of assuming this flick would be relatively benign (perhaps because they neglected to check out pluggedin.com first). The movie quickly turned a seedy corner. I'm proud to say that Kelsey walked out! Making this decision even more difficult was the fact that none of her girlfriends, all Christians, chose to do the same. That meant she had 90 minutes or so of "alone" time in the theater lobby.

Finally, there was the time Kelsey and a friend headed to another friend's home to watch a DVD. When they arrived they found out the group—including the parents—were switching from the positive movie they'd planned to view to a different flick—one with a lot of sexual joking and innuendo. Not one to make a scene, Kelsey quietly informed the friend and his parents that she preferred not to expose herself to the content, and found something else to do.

But the story isn't finished. A few days later, the mother told Kelsey how much she admired her for making that stand, adding something like, "We shouldn't have watched it either; it was really crude and trashy." In the interest of full disclosure: Please note that standing on principle doesn't always have the happy ending that this incident did.

I've included these stories from my daughter because they offer hope. If you feel you're constantly battling your kids over media boundaries, it can help to know that it really is possible to raise a child who desires to honor Christ with his or her entertainment choices—and that such a desire makes it much easier to set and maintain family standards.

It may also help to see this excerpt from a letter we received from a young man named Kenneth K.:

Personally I struggle with where the line needs to be drawn with the entertainment industry. The realization that there are two powers working in the world can be a tough pill to swallow. If I truly love God with all of me, I know that there is no way I can tolerate entertainment that defies who He is or what He stands for.

I would not go see a movie or listen to a song that mocks or bashes my earthly parents. If I saw a movie with great acting and an intelligent plot that was totally clean other than one mention of how much the main character hates my dad, I would not be able to look past that one part and say, "Well, other than one part, it was a great movie." Instead I would be angry because I love my father and I know of his love and the sacrifices he has made so that I can be where I am today. My hope is that I arrive at this place in my relationship with God. Trash in the entertainment industry offends me, but it doesn't bother me as much as I believe it should. I think I will become *more* offended as my walk with my Father and my King grows closer.

Like Kenneth, we need to realize that learning to see media from God's perspective is a process. Let's be encouraged by examples like Kenneth's—and be patient with ourselves and our kids as we journey in the same direction.

Lives do change. Hard hearts soften. Fighting over entertainment isn't inevitable. But in this media-saturated culture, it takes deliberate effort—an effort made easier when your kids want to love the Lord with all their heart, soul, mind, and strength.

Brian Welch:
A Change of Heart

In the late 90s, Korn ruled the pop charts with despairing nu-metal full of obscene, self-destructive lyrics. But in 2004, guitarist Brian "Head" Welch found himself at a crossroads, leaving the band and embracing Christ. He talked with me about his darkest days, his encounter with God, and the little girl who may have saved his life.

Q: Was leaving Korn a spiritual decision?

Brian: There was more than one reason I left that band. I wasn't into the music style and the direction they were going. The realness left a little bit, and the lyrics weren't all written by Korn members, which I didn't like. [But] one reason I'm not in the band anymore is that it's not God's plan for my life to be doing that.

Q: The primary factor was your young daughter, Jennea, wasn't it?

Brian: She was a big influence, such a pure, beautiful little girl. I would bring her on the road with me and see her getting corrupted by all the stuff that was going on. I'd try to hide it from her, but I couldn't. I was hooked on drugs, going into the bathroom snorting lines. Everyone's cussing, drinking, and smoking joints. I kept trying to ditch her to other people, like, "Raise my kid, I'm going to party." Then I'd come home strung out or hung over. I would want to be a good dad so bad, but I was so tired and selfish.

Q: In your book *Save Me from Myself,* you mention being disturbed to hear her singing a Korn song.

Brian: She was five years old, and I'm sitting there watching her sing, "All day I dream about sex" [from the song "A.D.I.D.A.S."]. That's not right. I don't care if she didn't know what she was singing. It still freaked me out. It's just not right for her to see her dad strung out on drugs, and it's not right for her to sing that song. It's like I was stealing her childhood or something, you know?

Q: Sure, but what about all the other Jenneas in the world who were into Korn's music? What about their innocence?

Brian: I didn't see that then. I didn't think about other people's kids. I figured parents would take care of their kids. When you don't have the Spirit of God you don't think about others; you just worry about yourself.

Q: With all of the entertainment targeting teens, which medium is most powerful?

Brian: I think it's still music. Video games and stuff like that you can play and it's a game—you turn into a robot. But music takes your emotions and your mind and it can change things and stir up things inside of you. It's really spiritual, putting music and words together.

Q: Let's talk about your conversion. How did God get your attention?

Brian: The last two years I was in Korn I partied nonstop and started doing speed every day. I got so addicted that I got scared. I tried to go to rehab, but that didn't work. No one could help me. Then I ended up seeing if Jesus was real, and He instantly took the drugs away. He revealed Himself to me and gave me the strength. Once I figured that out, I knew I was accountable to God.

Q: Who introduced you to the Lord?

Brian: All kinds of people had been asking me to go to different churches. I was just surrounded by Christians. One day I hooked up with these guys I was doing real estate with, and they invited me to their church. The pastor spoke about seeking first the kingdom of God, and all things and His righteousness will be given to you. I went home, sat down in my closet, and railed out all these lines. I started snorting them and said, "Jesus, take this stuff from me. I can't even quit. I want to quit so bad for my kid." A friend helped me throw all my stuff away. A week later I was just sitting at my computer, and I had this supernatural experience—an overwhelming sense of love not of this world—and I knew it was God. I changed my life right then.

Q: If you could tell teenagers one thing, what would it be?

Brian: I had everything in the world handed to me. I got to experience the top. Kids dream of becoming rock stars. I got it. It happened to me. I was a normal teen who had a hard time growing up and just happened to fall into this band that became huge. But if I compare it to my relationship with Christ and the destiny God has for me, it doesn't even compare to being with God. Anything you can gain from the world, if you aren't using it for God, it's just a waste of time. There's no purpose, no reason.

Q: Is music part of your new calling?

Brian: When I first got saved I was writing music that was really soft. I liked pleasant styles and wanted to chill out a little bit. Then one day I had this song and I just started screaming on it, and it came out awesome. So I felt like God was leading me to go back there. My music is real. It's about my experiences. It's genuine, really heavy rock music.

five

Preparing Them with Principles

As you can tell by reading this book, I'm passionate about encouraging followers of Christ to honor Him with their media choices. But I haven't always felt this way.

In fact, although I became a Christian at age 15, it wasn't until I was in my twenties that the Lord got through to me in this area. When I became a believer, there were a number of sins and habits that needed His lordship. Some necessary changes occurred almost instantly, but caring about obeying Him with my entertainment choices wasn't on the list.

So how did God get my attention concerning media? He finally got through my thick skull during the years I served as a youth pastor. Not through a sermon on purity or the need to be holy as He is holy. I'd heard and taught those topics many times. But for some reason I'd never felt they applied to entertainment.

Fortunately, a young man in my youth group gave me a cassette tape that addressed contemporary music and the need for discernment from a biblical perspective. Looking back, it seems strange that this particular teen would have handed me a teaching tape of any kind; he just wasn't the type. I have to think the Lord was leading him, since this must have been outside his comfort zone. He probably doesn't even remember doing it, but I've never forgotten.

Equally strange is the fact that I actually listened to this tape. I even played it the very day he gave it to me—a day the youth group took a ski trip on the church bus. As was my custom, we listened to a hard-rock station as far as the signal would reach. Then I stuck in this teaching cassette. The whole busload of passengers could have listened, too; whether anyone else was affected as I was is unclear to this day. But what I heard changed my life—and my calling.

As this Bible teacher spoke through the low-budget speakers of our bus, he combined biblical truth with real-life application, concentrating mostly on popular music and its influence. That mixture really convicted me.

In retrospect, I can see Bible verses alone hadn't gotten the job done for me because they hadn't seemed to apply. I needed to grasp what God's Word had to do with the dark music I'd championed for so many years. Once the speaker on this tape pointed this out and I grappled with the concept of honoring Christ with my musical selections, I was able to apply that to other forms of entertainment as well.

For me, the lightbulb had finally come on.

The Bible Tells Me So?

I think most believers—adults *and* kids—are like me in this: Before we'll get serious about improving our media diets, we need solid, well-documented, scriptural proof and the spiritual understanding of how these biblical principles apply to entertainment. Young people won't forgo the hottest TV sitcom, album, or Web site simply because their parents command it. Pretending otherwise only leads to more entertainment battles.

Kids want to know *why*. That requires specifics. Since listening to that tape, I've learned how many Scripture passages can be applied to media. If anything, I wish there were even more.

Far be it from me, of course, to try to tell the Lord how He could have made the Bible better. I'm absolutely convinced His Word is complete, infallible, and accurate—and doesn't need improvement of any kind. Yet I'll admit there are times I wish He'd included a few verses offering guidance on movie watching, channel surfing, DVD renting, video game playing, and music downloading—just to name a few media categories.

Somehow I imagine that if Jesus had spelled it out a bit more clearly in the Gospels, His followers would be more obedient in this area—and it wouldn't have taken me eight or so years to grasp it personally. I can't help but ponder the effect of a biblical narrative that might have gone something like this:

And as Jesus traveled further down the road, one of His disciples asked Him, "Lord, in the last days, what temptations will be snares to those who live on the earth?"

And Jesus replied, "There is coming a time when men, women, boys, and girls will stare for hours at moving images of people acting out all manner of evil that springs from man's heart. And at the same time, songs will be sung that despicably find false joy in perversion, violence, and darkness of all types.

"And people will laugh deeply at the evil they see and hear and desire to follow after this darkness. And when such darkness makes evil seem good and good seem evil, many in those days will rebel against their Creator with zeal. And many will follow after those behaviors and do likewise.

"But you, you should not succumb to these images or songs, laugh in your hearts at that evil, or partake of these forms of amusements. No, rather you should turn away from this darkness and during those days teach others how to stand against this vileness and in so doing, keep their hearts clean and pure for Me.

"And then there will come a day when something called a television . . ."

Unfortunately, for most of mankind's history such guidance wouldn't have made an ounce of sense to those who were reading it. *What's a television? What did Jesus mean when He spoke about MP3 downloading? What's an iPhone? The Internet? What did He mean when He spoke of slasher films and gangsta rap?*

Still, I can't help thinking that today's believers could benefit from some direct commands on these subjects. Not that God has been silent on the issue; it's just that the guidance isn't that low-hanging fruit so many of us prefer. One often needs a ladder to get it.

The Lord knew what He was doing when He decided that everything we need for that "lamp unto our feet" can be found within the pages of Scripture—even for modern issues such as today's entertainment. We won't find a "Thou shalt not use thy Facebook page to gossip or cast aspersions against thy neighbor" verse, but we'll find enough about loving our neighbor to know that gossiping about him or her is clearly a violation of God's goodness and commands. Whether gossip is spread face-to-face or computer to computer, the Lord's instructions remain the same.

That's also true about choosing the movies we watch. No, we won't find a "Thou shalt not view any R rated movie unless it be called *The Passion of the Christ*," but we'll find many principles that apply to what we allow into our hearts and minds.

So let's take a journey through several of those principles. Here are eight you can share with your kids—and apply together to media choices.

Pass-along Principle #1: Avoid Pollution

James, the half-brother of Jesus Himself, explains what true religion looks like: "Religion that God our Father accepts as pure and faultless is this: to look after orphans and widows in their distress . . ." (James 1:27).

Most sermons you've heard about widows and orphans probably stopped there. But the verse keeps going. James adds, "and to keep oneself from being polluted by the world."

A note in *The Full Life Study Bible* explains the passage this way: "James gives two principles that define the content of true Christianity . . . [the second being] keeping ourselves holy before God. James says that love for others must be accompanied by a love for God expressed in separation from the world's sinful ways. Love for others must be accompanied by holiness before God or it is not Christian love."[1]

Did you catch that old-fashioned-sounding phrase, "separation from the world's sinful ways"? It may be hard to swallow these days, but James is saying that true religion involves staying away from certain things so that we can achieve the goal of not being polluted by evil.

The application to entertainment is obvious, but not always easy. Separation can be taken to an unhealthy extreme; we're not to be *of* the world, but are still supposed to live *in* it (see John 17:14-16). The "not of it" part calls us to be different, refusing to enjoy the darkness others may find amusing.

The apostle Paul weighs in with this instruction:

> For what do righteousness and wickedness have in common? Or what fellowship can light have with darkness? . . . Therefore come out from them and be separate, says the Lord. Touch no unclean thing, and I will receive you. I will be a Father to you, and you will be my sons and daughters, says the Lord Almighty. Since we have these promises, dear friends, let us purify ourselves from everything that contaminates body and spirit, perfecting holiness out of reverence for God. (2 Corinthians 6:14, 17–7:1)

Many kids (and adults) find it hard to be separate when it comes to media because they're much more concerned about what their friends might think than they are about honoring Christ and pleasing Him. Given a choice, they'd rather separate themselves from a close relationship with God than from their peers. That seemed to be the attitude of Laura, who sent us this e-mail:

> To Whom It May Concern:
> You ruin the lives of many teenagers with conservative Christian parents. I am not immoral, and I know the difference between right and wrong. I have seen many of the movies that you review, and in these reviews, you overreact and make huge deals about things that are so insignificant. I am 18 years old and will be a senior in high school. However, I am restricted to the freedoms

of a 10 year old when it comes to watching movies because of my parents' religious reading of the reviews written by your uptight staff who only approve of *Narnia* and *Facing the Giants*. I would greatly appreciate if they would cease including their own opinions in their reviews. They are not God, and just because they say something is inappropriate does not mean that it actually is. . . . Please tell [your reviewer] that tomorrow night I will be forced to stay home, while my friends, including the daughter of a pastor, will be viewing the "graphic sexual content" in the movie [I want so badly to attend]. I am sure they will all come back scarred for life. Thank you for preserving my innocence. So I guess I'll just stay home and watch *Shrek the Third*. . . .

Most sincerely,
Laura

If you have a teenager who seems to lean in Laura's direction, take hope in the fact that people can change. I did, and so have many, many others.

In my case, I needed to be convinced that God really cared about this area. I'd probably read through the New Testament a half-dozen times without connecting it to media issues. That tape helped make the connection.

Perhaps that's what it will take to get your young person's attention—specifics about media influence, evidence from researchers, testimonies from those who get it, and learning from the mistakes of those who don't. Combine these with lots of prayer, the right moments to talk about this issue—and who knows what the Lord might do?

Pass-along Principle #2: Choose Your Friends Carefully
One of my favorite Bible chapters offering a media-related principle is Psalm 1:

Blessed is the man who does not walk in the counsel of the wicked or stand in the way of sinners or sit in the seat of mockers. But his delight is in the law of the Lord, and on his law he meditates day and night. He is like a tree planted by streams of water, which yields its fruit in season and whose leaf does not wither. Whatever he does prospers. Not so the wicked! They are like chaff that the wind blows away. (Psalm 1:1-4)

How is this media-related? After all, when King David penned these words, I'm sure that even in his wildest imagination he couldn't have envisioned movie theaters, DVD players, smart phones, the Internet, video games, and 1,350-channel television programming. When he warned us not to hang out with mockers, he was thinking face-to-face.

Today we can hang out with people without ever going near them. We can vote with them in response to a "reality" show, argue with them on an Internet comments page, share photos with them on a social networking site, and challenge them to an online gaming duel. We can spend hours with heroes, villains, pundits, and gurus on big screens and small.

Not all of these "someones" are problematic. But quite a number qualify. Being careful about who influences us takes time and thought. Does your child know how to evaluate potential friends? How about the musicians, actors, characters, and Web surfers he or she may spend hours with?

Help your child understand why the writer of Proverbs advises us to choose our companions carefully. He says it this way: "Do not make friends with a hot-tempered man, do not associate with one easily angered, or you may learn his ways and get yourself ensnared" (Proverbs 22:24).

The writer also warns not to "envy a violent man or choose any of his ways" (Proverbs 3:31). How might this apply to shoot-'em-up video games, vengeful song lyrics, or the *Saw* films? Avoiding brutal forms of entertainment—and those who encourage us to join in—will make it much easier to follow Christ's teachings about loving enemies and turning the other cheek.

Pass-along Principle #3: Escape from Captivity

Another powerful principle that can prepare your kids to learn media discernment is found in Colossians 2:8: "See to it that no one takes you captive through hollow and deceptive philosophy, which depends on human tradition and the basic principles of the world rather than on Christ."

Every movie and television script, every video game story line, and every song is based on someone's philosophy. Not all entertainment is "hollow and deceptive," of course. But much of it is, and many kids willingly allow themselves to be taken captive. The process occurs slowly—a gradual desensitization. For these young people, enjoying something they can see or hear now seems much more real than the unseen things of God. They sell their birthright, if you will, for today's media porridge—because the latter seems tastier than the flavor of doing things His way.

If you're wondering what it looks like for a person to be taken captive by false and deceptive philosophies, consider a young man named Andrew who sent us this message:

> First I would like to state that I am a hip-hop and all around music fan. Second I would like to state that Mr. Bob Waliszewski is a blatant moron who does not have any business writing these reviews. The man is clearly not a fan of hip-hop one bit and throws the term "gangsta rap" on everything. . . . His reviews are strictly about the words, not the art. These reviews seem to be directed towards an audience of parents buying their children presents. I don't know why he even reviews hip-hop albums if he is just going to call all of them "lewd."
>
> . . . If Bob smoked pot he would have a much greater appreciation for what [one of my favorite musicians] does. . . . I honestly hate you Mr. Bob. You just ruined my day.

I don't take any joy in ruining anyone's day. I'm actually a fan of hip-hop music; there are artists in this genre, primarily Christians, who know how to craft songs that encourage and inspire. It's fair to say that I review entertainment because of parents and their children. But it's not to ruin their fun; it's to speak the truth in love to a world that desperately needs it.

Andrew's message reflects more than one deceptive philosophy. Apparently he's bought the argument that lyrics don't matter, only "art" does. Aren't lyrics part of the art? He seems to think that only those he regards as fans of a genre should be allowed to comment on it. And even though he's being sarcastic, to some degree he may believe that using illegal drugs enhances art appreciation.

Pass-along Principle #4: Discover the Joys of Self-denial

Some concepts about God bring smiles to our children's faces. Tell them they're special in God's eyes and that they're fearfully and wonderfully made; you'll get no frowns. The same goes for having a God-designed ultimate purpose. But tell them about God's call to self-denial, and you'll get a furrowed brow.

It's in the Bible, though. We mustn't overlook training our children about it and its benefits. Jesus in Luke 9:23 explains, "If anyone would come after me, he must deny himself and take up his cross daily and follow me."

I've found over the years that the message of honoring Christ with our entertainment choices doesn't always play well in the church, especially among teenagers. That's because we can't discuss the subject without emphasizing the concept that we may have to *deny* ourselves something "fun" while others don't. The mere idea that self-denial may be the best way to live appears excessively painful and distressing.

I know how that feels. Probably all of us have been tempted to skip over Bible passages like this one. It's as if we wish Jesus had said, "If anyone would follow after Me, let him indulge himself and not worry about taking up a cross of sacrifice. After all, I'm really here to help you have a good time and make your happiness My highest priority."

The Lord *does* care about our happiness and well-being. Ultimately, though, we get there not by amusing ourselves but through taking up our cross, denying ourselves, and following Him.

Our children need to understand this and see us model self-denial. Do they see us decline that raunchy PG-13 movie? Do they see us change the radio dial when an inappropriate tune comes on? If asked by their friends if their parents watch a popular, off-color television program, could they honestly answer, "No"?

Pass-along Principle #5: Put a Guard on Your Heart

As I've mentioned before, Proverbs 4:23 reminds us, "Above all else, guard your heart, for it is the wellspring of life."

It takes action to guard our heart; it doesn't just happen. As spiritual as it may sound, we can't just pray a guarded heart into being: "God, I'm about to go to this R rated movie, so please protect my mind." It doesn't work that way.

Guarding something means carefully choosing the things we let inside. That's extra hard with entertainment, since it often bombards us at an emotional level—a level at which we're most vulnerable.

Suppose you're in college. Your professor is very pro-evolution but you're not. Since you know the subject is bound to come up, when he starts talking about Darwin you instantly put up your guard. You're not buying a thing he says until he gets on to another subject.

But entertainment works differently. Because we're consuming for our enjoyment, we automatically let our heart's guard down. As we laugh and enjoy what we're seeing and hearing, our unguarded heart is much more likely to embrace ideas and concepts that a guarded heart would reject.

Long before the invention of television, cell phone touchscreens, or movie projectors, King David wisely wrote, "I will set before my eyes no vile thing" (Psalm 101:3). Can you imagine how it would change the world if believers around the globe applied this passage to entertainment viewing?

A friend of mine believes we should all write this verse on card stock and place it on or above our TVs. Not a bad idea! Try making some cards like that as a family project—not just for TVs but for computers, too.

Pass-along Principle #6: Make Wisdom Your Goal

Here's an amazing but true story to tell your kids.

One night in a dream, the Lord appeared to Solomon and gave him the fantastic opportunity to ask for anything he wished (1 Kings 3:4-10). Rather than asking for fame, fortune, or the defeat of his enemies, Solomon requested a "discerning heart" and the ability to "distinguish between right and wrong." The Lord was so pleased with Solomon's request that He gave him not only discernment but the other things, too.

No doubt it took a bit of wisdom to ask for wisdom. What if your child's main goal was a "discerning heart"? What would it look like if this discernment were applied toward media?

The first step to getting there is asking, even as Solomon did. Might you suggest this prayer request to your children? Perhaps they have not because they've asked not.

And don't forget that a little discernment leads to more. In other words, we don't get the whole ball of wax at once; it comes in stages. Proverbs 4:18 says it this way: "The path of the righteous is like the first gleam of dawn, shining ever brighter till the full light of day."

I like the idea of "ever brighter." It gives me hope that the brightness I—and my family—now walk in will seem dim a decade from now. Or at least it should!

Pass-along Principle #7: Think Different

Even if your kids are young, they probably need to learn new ways of thinking about the things they've seen and heard in the media. We all do. Here's Paul's reminder:

> You were taught, with regard to your former way of life, to put
> off your old self, which is being corrupted by its deceitful desires;
> to be made new in the attitude of your minds; and to put on the
> new self, created to be like God in true righteousness and holiness.
> (Ephesians 4:22-24)

Putting off our old selves and getting new minds is made tougher when we pay little attention to our entertainment decisions. Or to put it another way, it's much easier to accomplish those goals when our minds are saturated with God's ideas and not Hollywood's.

The notion of having a new attitude was so important to Paul that he brought it up when writing to the Romans, too: "Do not conform any longer to the pattern of this world, but be transformed by the renewing of your mind" (Romans 12:2). It's hard to follow Paul's advice when we allow our brains to dwell on the "old nature's" cravings and assumptions—an area in which the media truly deserve a case full of trophies.

Your kids need to know that if they belong to Jesus, they have weapons—spiritual ones—that can make the mind renewal process easier. Here's Paul again:

> For though we live in the world, we do not wage war as the world
> does. The weapons we fight with are not the weapons of the world.
> On the contrary, they have divine power to demolish strongholds.
> We demolish arguments and every pretension that sets itself up
> against the knowledge of God, and we take captive every thought
> to make it obedient to Christ. (2 Corinthians 10:3-5)

I love this passage. Clearly, it says we can *do* something. We're not victims who have to fall helplessly into embracing the values of this world. We can take a wrecking ball to false fronts that pose as firm foundations. I, for one, am glad our families don't have to wave the white flag when half-truths come knocking on our brains for acceptance.

Pass-along Principle #8: Expect a Struggle

Let's be honest with our kids. None of this is easy. And these principles usually are grasped over time, not instantly. I don't believe we ever gain total dominance over the troubling thoughts, media-inspired or not, that invade our thinking.

Paul illustrated this when he discussed his own battle:

> We know that the law is spiritual; but I am unspiritual, sold as a
> slave to sin. I do not understand what I do. For what I want to do

I do not do, but what I hate I do. . . . I know that nothing good
lives in me, that is, in my sinful nature. For I have the desire to do
what is good, but I cannot carry it out. (Romans 7:14-15, 18)

What? *Paul?* He wasn't unspiritual, was he? He was a spiritual
giant!

Well, yes and no. By his own admission he was also confused, and
no doubt frustrated at times, with the things he found himself doing
and failing to do. Our kids need to know that.

They also need to know that Paul's story didn't end there. He also
found hope and freedom:

Who will rescue me from this body of death? Thanks be to God—
through Jesus Christ our Lord! So then, I myself in my mind am
a slave to God's law, but in the sinful nature a slave to the law of
sin. Therefore, there is now no condemnation for those who are in
Christ Jesus, because through Christ Jesus the law of the Spirit of
life set me free from the law of sin and death. (Romans 7:24–8:2)

Fighting that inner battle didn't keep Paul from maintaining and
promoting standards. In Ephesians 5:3-4 he told believers that there
shouldn't be even a "hint of sexual immorality, or of any kind of impurity" among them. He turned thumbs down on "obscenity, foolish
talk or coarse joking" in their midst. And in Ephesians 5:11 he writes,
"Have nothing to do with the fruitless deeds of darkness, but rather
expose them."

Do you struggle with entertainment choices? Don't let your
imperfections keep you from addressing this topic with your kids. Be
the best example you can, but don't give up when you slip. Be honest
about your mistakes, and keep pointing your children (and yourself)
to the Bible's standards.

That may mean your family stays home on a Friday night when
everyone else is heading off to the theater. Or buying an E rated video
game when everyone else is playing the hottest M rated one.

If you've prepared your kids for times like that, you'll be less likely to ignite the next World War. That means teaching them, both casually and formally, principles like the ones in this chapter. Paul tells Timothy he needs to "train [himself] to be godly" (1 Timothy 4:7). As in athletics, training is necessary. That means hard work and perseverance—followed by more training.

But also as with athletics, getting in spiritual shape offers an ocean of rewards.

Some Verses to Memorize

Here are a few scriptures your young person may find helpful as he or she trains to be more media-savvy. You might even want to commit some of them to memory together.

Above all else, guard your heart, for it is the wellspring of life. (Proverbs 4:23)

Put away perversity from your mouth; keep corrupt talk far from your lips. (Proverbs 4:24)

Blessed is the man who does not walk in the counsel of the wicked or stand in the way of sinners or sit in the seat of mockers. But his delight is in the law of the LORD, and on his law he meditates day and night. (Psalm 1:1-2)

If anyone would come after me, he must deny himself and take up his cross daily and follow me. (Luke 9:23)

You were taught, with regard to your former way of life, to put off your old self, which is being corrupted by its deceitful desires. (Ephesians 4:22)

My son, preserve sound judgment and discernment, do not let them out of your sight. (Proverbs 3:21)

The weapons we fight with are not the weapons of the world. On the contrary, they have divine power to demolish strongholds. We demolish arguments and every pretension that sets itself up against the knowledge of God, and we take captive every thought to make it obedient to Christ. (2 Corinthians 10:4-5)

I will set before my eyes no vile thing. The deeds of faithless men I hate; they will not cling to me. (Psalm 101:3)

For out of the overflow of the heart the mouth speaks. The good man brings good things out of the good stored up in him, and the evil man brings evil things out of the evil stored up in him. But I tell you that men will have to give account on the day of judgment for every careless word they have spoken. (Matthew 12:34-36)

Have nothing to do with the fruitless deeds of darkness, but rather expose them. (Ephesians 5:11)

Do not conform any longer to the pattern of this world, but be transformed by the renewing of your mind. (Romans 12:2)

See to it that no one takes you captive through hollow and deceptive philosophy, which depends on human tradition and the basic principles of this world rather than on Christ. (Colossians 2:8)

Finally, brothers, whatever is true, whatever is noble, whatever is right, whatever is pure, whatever is lovely, whatever is admirable—if anything is excellent or praiseworthy—think about such things. (Philippians 4:8)

six

Ten Things You Can Do to End Fights over Family Entertainment

Remember "John" from Chapter 1?

He was the dad who wanted me to referee the battle that erupted when he demanded that his 15-year-old daughter stop watching a Disney Channel program that made him uncomfortable—even though he didn't know much about it.

"I just don't like the boy-girl thing" on that show, he said.

His daughter burst into tears and his wife took the daughter's side. I was supposed to break the tie between the spouses.

What do you think? Was John right in asking his daughter to turn the program off? Was his wife overreacting?

The Verdict

My friend John wanted me to say, "You were right in having your daughter turn off the TV," but I didn't see it that way. In fact, a much bigger problem was developing in his home, and I told him so.

He risked alienating his daughter by barking out orders, without showing fatherly affection and without communicating how his deep love for Christ was his underlying motivation. In fact, I'm not really certain his love for the Lord *was* his main motivation. I think it was more along the lines of, "I don't want my daughter being promiscuous, and this television show certainly doesn't support purity."

As it turned out, the program that concerned John was rather innocuous. It wasn't perfect, but it didn't justify his knee-jerk reaction. I advised him to record a few episodes and watch with his daughter, explaining any concerns he might have.

Most of all, though, John needed to make sure his daughter knew how much he valued her. He needed to explain that having media rules in their home was a natural expression of that love. He also needed to admit that although the driving force behind his actions may have been noble, his execution was lacking. That led to one more need: to apologize.

John's overreaction to his daughter's television viewing is a reminder that even though training our children to be savvy about entertainment is an important life skill, any attempt to achieve that harshly with unexplained, stern boundaries is counterproductive.

When done right, teaching discernment helps our kids make better choices for a lifetime, not just while they live under our roof. That's important because new entertainment arrives daily, and delivery gizmos and gadgets change almost as rapidly. Yet no matter what tops the charts or what systems are used to enjoy it, John's situation shows that even the best rules must be enforced with love.

Whether or not you've ever had a similar run-in with your son or daughter, consider using the record-watch-and-discuss method I suggested to John. In other words, enter your child's entertainment world. Become familiar with his or her favorites and those of his or her friends, and why these are high on the list. There's no need to view your child's media consumption as some secret place with a large No Parents Allowed sign above the entrance. Give yourself permission to enter—gently and lovingly.

Top Ten Tips

Other than entering your child's media world, how can you help him or her plot a course through today's entertainment and technological land mines—without wrecking your relationship? Using love as a guide, I'd like to suggest 10 practical steps you can take.

Tip #1: Make Decisions Based on God's View

I was hanging out with some Christian friends awhile back, and as so often happens, the conversation turned to movies including an objectionable R rated one. I was told to plug my ears so that I wouldn't be offended by one friend's positive perspective on the film.

I simply noted, "It doesn't matter what I think, it matters what the Lord thinks." Fortunately, this person took this comment in the spirit in which I intended it—not cutting or condemning, but thought-provoking. He would later tell me that my words helped him make changes to his viewing habits.

Our thoughts about media consumption should be determined by God's thoughts, not the other way around. Although this idea is straightforward, my experience tells me that living it out can be tricky because many people of faith consider only this: *Do I think I will* enjoy *this movie, show, Web site, video game, song, book, or magazine?*

That's not to say that making good media decisions is easy. Even strong, mature believers find navigating the murky waters a bit of a gray area. I'll admit I'm a black-and-white sort of person called to make judgment calls about often-cloudy media. I much prefer subjects that clearly are right or wrong, in bounds or out, positive or negative. Today's entertainment often doesn't fit neatly into those categories.

For instance, should a single profanity be reason enough for a 17-year-old to avoid a certain movie? What about for a seven-year-old? How much violence is too much? Is an hour a day of video gaming excessive? Even among well-meaning Christians, there is no consensus.

I do believe, though, that while God wants us to be happy, on a narrow mountain pass *holiness* has the right-of-way. Jesus said, "If you love me, you will obey what I command" (John 14:15). He also pointed out that those who follow Him should "deny" themselves and take up their cross (Luke 9:23). Obedience is God's priority. As your children embrace this concept it will help them say "no" to troublesome media products—even when their friends are saying "yes." When being entertained is valued more highly than honoring the Lord, we've strayed into dangerous—and contentious—territory.

Tip #2: Teach WWJD

It's Friday night. The long-awaited, certain-to-be-a-box-office-smash starts playing every 30 minutes at the local theater. Your oldest is begging to go because "all" his friends will be there. Your daughter's been invited to a slumber party where some romantic comedy is the big draw. Your youngest is raving about a hot new band his buddies like. You just want to kick back with your spouse, pop some popcorn, and watch a new pay-per-view movie.

How do you and your family make decisions about these entertainment opportunities and know in your heart you've made the right ones? Is there a straightforward guideline all of you can agree to follow?

While there are factors like age appropriateness, spiritual maturity, and the possibility of being a "stumbling block" to a brother (Romans 14:13), I think the lion's share of media choices can be made by asking the question popularized more than a decade ago by the WWJD (What Would Jesus Do?) bracelets. The fad may be passé, but the principle behind it will never fade.

I actually prefer an expanded version of the question, something like this: If Jesus were walking the planet today with His 12 disciples, how would He respond if Peter, John, or Matthew asked, "Can we go see or listen to [fill in the blank here]?" Or "How about if we play this video game?"

These are questions we should always ask before choosing entertainment. And they're questions we need to train our kids to ask as well.

Help your son or daughter understand that Christ's answer to these questions would be based entirely upon His *love* for His disciples, not on a desire to squelch their fun. None of us knows what Jesus would do or say in every situation, but it's our job to train our kids to prayerfully seek what He *likely* would do based on His holiness and character.

Tip #3: Instill Biblical Principles

Peter, James, John, Abraham, and Moses didn't have to worry about what movies their sons might watch, what songs the DJ at the high school dance would be spinning, or what TV shows their daughters might be watching on their cell phones. Nor did they face the challenges of texting, YouTube, Facebook, Twitter, Second Life, Hulu, or Pandora.

But as I've already mentioned, even though the Bible never says, "Thou shalt not listen to gangsta rap," it's full of passages to help us navigate the culture. It's the place to go when you're looking for authoritative answers—a much better place than "Because I said so" or "You're embarrassing me in front of all the other parents at church."

Your kids may not be used to consulting Scripture about their media choices. After all, 91 percent of teens who say they're "born again" make moral decisions by means other than God's absolute truth; most say they use their "feelings."[1] But it's a habit you can encourage, and one that might even help prevent media battles that arise when parents and kids rely solely on personal preferences and opinions.

How can you help your children form that habit of thinking biblically about topics like entertainment? If your kids are preteens or teens, here's one way:

> *Appoint an ethics chair.* Some universities create a "chair," or office of a designated expert, on issues like ethics. You can do the same at home, naming one of the chairs at your dinner table the "ethics chair." Let a different person sit in the chair each night for a week; he or she is to weigh in on the right and wrong of subjects discussed at the table. Other family members are free to talk about ethics too, but the "chairperson" makes sure that at least one moral issue is raised at each meal. If your "expert" takes a questionable stand, resist the urge to overrule him; simply ask him to explain how his position fits with what the Bible says.[2]

Tip #4: Model It

Nothing spoils the effectiveness of a media discernment message like a parent who doesn't practice what he or she preaches. If your child knows you're not applying those principles to your own entertainment choices, you're asking for a fight. Most kids—especially teenagers—know hypocrisy when they see it, and they don't respect it.

But no earthly parent is perfectly consistent. So how can you be a walking advertisement for making good entertainment choices? Author and pastor Chip Ingram knows the importance of modeling, but encourages us not to expect the impossible from ourselves:

> Can you imagine lining your children up on the couch, looking them in the eye, and saying: "I want you to be like me. I want you to talk the way I talk, drive the way I drive, eat and drink the way I eat and drink, watch the kinds of shows I watch, handle your money like I handle my money, balance work and rest like I balance work and rest, and handle your anger like I handle mine"? Would you be comfortable giving them that kind of charge? If not, the most profound parenting decision you will ever make may be how you respond to what you just read.
>
> Can you fathom the lifelong difference you could make in your children's lives if you stopped right now to identify the attributes that you're uncomfortable passing down to them and then systematically began to allow those attributes to be conformed to Christ? You must become who you want your children to become.
>
> If a responsibility that heavy causes you to feel an enormous amount of pressure, let me encourage you. You don't have to be perfect. In fact, you couldn't pass perfection down to your kids if you wanted to; they're fallen human beings, just like you and me. What you *can* do, however, is demonstrate how godly people handle themselves when they blow it. Authenticity is the goal, not perfection. Let them see how you deal with failure as well as how you deal with success. You can demonstrate what it means

to repent, to confess, to humbly accept responsibility for your mistakes, and to ask forgiveness. In fact, asking your child to forgive you for a mistake is one of the most powerful teaching tools you have. It's not about having it all together; it's about living out what you believe day by day and responding appropriately when you miss the mark. It's impossible for you to be perfect for your kids, but *anyone* can be authentic.[3]

Let your kids see you making media decisions. If you can't explain why it's okay for you to rent that DVD or download that song or frequent that Web site, you may need to make a better choice. Being as consistent as you can gives your kids one less thing to argue about.

Tip #5: Get Your Pastors On Board

When your kids hear other people—pastors, parents, teachers—echoing your advice on media, they may be more willing to listen.

Encourage your youth pastor to schedule a parent/teen night to discuss the subject of honoring Christ with entertainment decisions. Ask the head of your children's ministry whether making good media choices could be part of the curriculum in Sunday school or children's church. Talk to your senior pastor about including this subject in his plans; a sermon or two each year goes a long way.

Tip #6: Develop a Family Media Constitution

It's one thing to talk about media discernment. It's another thing to spell out expectations in writing.

A written family media constitution placed in a prominent place serves as a constant reminder of its importance. I'd also suggest exploring this issue in your family devotions or family meetings at least twice a year.

I'll have more to say on this subject in the next chapter. For now, you might start thinking about forming a constitutional committee—and considering what your family believes is most valuable, enjoyable, and hazardous about entertainment.

Tip #7: Encourage Positive Alternatives

Our Creator is not anti-entertainment. The arts and media are not inherently evil. It's a rare individual God calls to throw out the television, listen to music written only by Handel, and never darken the door of the neighborhood theater or video store.

Few families can set and maintain such austere media boundaries successfully. Many (though not all) who go this route just give their kids ammunition for rebellion—especially when they leave home for college or jobs. I'm convinced the workable approach for most of us is to find constructive entertainment alternatives.

I don't mean that entertainment has to be "Christian" to get a thumbs-up. There are really three types of artistic expression: positive (which generally includes media with a Christian worldview), neutral, and objectionable. The first two are those we should seek; the latter is the type we should avoid.

Just what do I mean by these three classifications? Positive entertainment is that which inspires, uplifts, encourages, and motivates the listener or viewer to do something to make this world, another individual, or oneself better. It might be a song that promotes forgiveness, condemns spousal abuse, or gives a boost to volunteerism. It might be a television program that highlights the joy of remodeling someone's dilapidated home to make it more wheelchair accessible for an occupant.

Objectionable entertainment is the opposite. Examples abound as this type promotes pride, selfishness, immorality, rebellion, greed, and drug use—often portraying these behaviors as glamorous, fun, and beneficial.

How about "neutral" entertainment? I'll explain it this way: On the music side of things, think of a song with lyrics that might go something like, "I looked into her eyes, and she in mine/And we walked along the beach hand in hand." These love-lines aren't going to bring about world peace, but there's nothing wrong with the ideas being advanced here, either.

With these categories in mind, discuss as a family what constitutes suitable positive and neutral entertainment—and how to find those types.

Tip #8: Consider "Movie Nights"

Focus on the Family has published three *Movie Nights* books, exploring quality mainstream films you can watch with your kids as a fun launchpad for positive, healthy discussion afterward. Newer, printable versions of many *Movie Nights* discussion guides are available at pluggedin.com for use with both teens and young children, and more are being added regularly.

Think of *Movie Nights* as mini-curricula designed to help families talk about spiritual truth, using the "parables" found in certain popular films. For example, here are a few of the discussion questions for *Toy Story 2* listed in the book *Movie Nights for Kids*:

- When Andy leaves Woody behind, Woody dreams that Andy says, "You're broken. I don't want to play with you anymore." How do most kids tend to treat others who have something "wrong" with them? Read Matthew 25:31-40. How do you think God wants us to treat people who are "broken"?
- Wheezy the Penguin, put on the shelf because his squeaker doesn't work, says, "We're all just one stitch away" from being sold in a yard sale. What do you think he means? Is this how God feels about us, always ready to punish us or throw us away if we don't please Him? Read 1 John 1:9 and 1 John 4:16-19 to find out.
- When Al does that last commercial in his chicken suit, why is he crying? If things had turned out differently and he'd sold Woody and the other toys, do you think he would have been happy? For how long? Read Jesus' story about the greedy man in Luke 12:15-21. How is this man like Al?[4]

There are even suggestions for a pre-film field trip to the toy store, a post-movie service project (giving away toys no longer used) and photo treasure hunt (taking pictures of the most valuable things in your home—people), plus behind-the-scenes trivia about two voices featured in the film. That beats arguing about movies any day! To try a "movie night" with your kids, go to pluggedin.com, pick a film, and print out a discussion guide.

Tip #9: Use the Buddy System

My own daughter, who is now serving with her youth pastor husband, honed her discernment skills by teaching the subject to elementary students in our church. But before grabbing the microphone, she latched on to a best friend in high school, a girl who shared her commitment to honor the Lord in this area. They found it much easier to walk this path together than alone. Together iron sharpened iron (Proverbs 27:17).

Friends like that aren't always easy to find. But it's worth trying to help your son or daughter seek "iron" in his or her life, too. When your child hears from a peer that media discernment has value, you may feel less under siege—and less prone to slip into battle mode.

Tip #10: Avoid Extremes

Many parents take an "all or nothing" approach, rather than teaching and reinforcing biblical principles on a case-by-case basis. These moms and dads tend to swing to one extreme or the other—something that's easy to do.

The first extreme is permissiveness. Some parents seemingly can't say no to their children. They so much want to be liked by their kids that they seldom risk setting limits. They adopt an "anything goes" philosophy: No boundaries, everything is okay, do what you want. This approach leads to "indecent exposure" as children wander, aimless and wide-eyed, through the culture's enticements. We must not make this common mistake; we have to be parents who know how and when to say no.

The other extreme is legalism. Parents at this end of the spectrum rarely explain their decisions, but find the first thing out of their mouths is "No."

"Dad, can I go to XYZ movie?"

"No!"

"Can I listen to contemporary Christian music?"

"No!"

"Mom, can I buy a video game console?"

"No!"

This type of parenting purports to be about safeguarding. It isn't.

This approach may simplify entertainment purchasing decisions, but it also can breed rebellion. Youngsters often bide their time, waiting for the day they can sample the entertainment industry's forbidden fruit: "Just wait 'til I move out someday. I'll watch and listen to whatever I want." When they head off to college or career, this attitude may play out in unwise choices. That's why we also need to be parents who can say yes when it's warranted.

Neither of the extremes works. A discerning middle ground—one that tests entertainment against biblical standards—is the most reasonable and protective plan of action. Teaching discernment encourages balance, leads to critical thinking, bonds families, and gives teens life skills they'll carry throughout adulthood.

Talking Your Way Through Conflict

Disagreements aren't the same as fights, and the former don't have to lead to the latter. That's true when it comes to hairstyles and junk food, and it's true where media choices are concerned.

How can you pour oil on the troubled waters of an entertainment-related conflict? Authors Joe White and Lissa Johnson, in their book *Sticking with Your Teen*, offer the following advice. If your child isn't a teenager yet, don't worry. Most of the tips are adaptable to raising younger children—and even to keeping the peace with spouses.

Confrontations happen in practically every home, but they're guaranteed when you and your teen aren't close. How can you communicate in a way that helps you reconnect?

Here are a dozen tips for talking your way through conflict:

1. *Start strong.* Psychologists say the first three minutes of a conversation generally dictate how the rest of it will go. Begin a confrontation with a soft voice and respect for your teen, and it's likely that the confrontation will be more productive and less destructive. As one teen testifies, "My mom and I had effective communication because I was treated as an equal. Not in terms of who was in charge (that was clear) but in that I had a voice."

2. *Let your teen speak first.* Young people we surveyed said that if they have a chance to talk first, they're more receptive to what their parents say. Once teens get to speak their minds, they're usually willing to listen to the other side.

3. *Don't interrupt.* It's tempting to dive in and react to a piece of what your teen just said, but one girl described how that looks from her point of view: "My parents interrupt me and lecture/yell. Then while they're talking and I want to get a word in, I'm yelled at for interrupting. It's really unfair." If either of you tends to talk nonstop, set a timer for two or three minutes and take turns.

4. *Watch your tone of voice and body language.* Model what you want your teen to do. When parents yell or use sarcasm or point fingers, kids figure it's okay for them to do the same. They also put on their protective gear and get into "fight" position. If you turn angry, use a quieter, calmer voice. If nothing else, your teen will have to listen harder to hear you.

5. *Explain what you want and why.* Some teens say they just don't understand what their parents are asking them to do. Have your teen restate what you've told him. Explain the reasons for your request or rule. For example: "I understand you'd like to be with your friends at the concert. But you've been out late every night this week and you can hardly get out of bed in the morning. That's not good for you, or for your schoolwork. Maybe next time."

6. *Fight fair.* No name-calling. Stick to the issue at hand. Don't dredge up past failures. Avoid the words "always" and "never," and don't compare your teen with anyone—living or dead, related or unrelated.

7. *Don't beat your teen over the head with Bible verses or biblical concepts.* Sure, it's crucial to pass principles from God's Word on to your child. But most arguments don't qualify as "teachable moments." Your teen won't be too receptive if you declare, "I don't care if it makes you look like a nerd! You'll wear that orange sweater to school because the Bible says to obey your parents. Besides, vanity is a sin!"

8. *Give weight to your teen's feelings and opinions.* You may think it's just "realistic" to tell your teen, "So, the girls said mean things about you. Forget it. You have to get used to people doing that." Instead of feeling like you've just prepared her for the real world, though, your teen will feel dismissed and misunderstood.

9. *Don't try to control your teen's side of the confrontation.* It doesn't work! Let's say your teen is "sassing" you. You could retort, "You will not talk to me like that!" Not a good move, since a statement like this challenges him to prove he, not you, controls his tongue. Instead you could say, "I'll be happy to listen to you when you speak to me more respectfully." Now you're saying what *you* will do—something you *can* control.

10. *Keep the issues in perspective.* How important is this fight, anyway? Is it possible to work toward a win-win solution, or at least one everybody can live with? Are you choosing your battles wisely? Stand up for the values that are most important to you and to your teen's welfare—but consider flexibility on lesser matters.

11. *Take a break when necessary.* If you or your teen are getting too wound up, take a time out. It doesn't hurt to put a conflict on the back burner until people calm down.

12. *When talking fails, write a letter.* Writing gives you time to sort through your thoughts and express yourself carefully. It gives your teen time to respond instead of reacting defensively. A notebook passed back and forth can work, too; so does e-mail. That's what a mom and dad discovered when their 13-year-old son wanted to see an R-rated movie; they kept telling him no, and he kept arguing. Finally Mom wrote him an e-mail, explaining their reasons. The boy never asked about it again, and seemed warmer toward his parents than he'd been in quite a while.[5]

Disagreements can be healthy. Your whole family can grow closer by dealing thoughtfully and lovingly with media-related differences of opinion. One powerful way to do that is by writing a family entertainment constitution—as you'll see in the next chapter.

seven

Your Family Entertainment Constitution

Recently I hired a professional paint contractor I'd never met. I'd never even heard the company's name.

The first time I ever saw the owner of the company was when she pulled up in my driveway. We walked around my house while I explained what I wanted, pointing out aspects of my home's exterior that needed attention. She called back a day later, quoted me a price over the phone, and I agreed to it. Nothing was put in writing.

Fortunately, everything worked out all right. But I don't recommend doing business this way! I knew it could have been disastrous. Yet I didn't insist on a written contract, nor did the painter ask me to sign something in which I agreed to her terms.

Perhaps you're thinking, *Why would he do this?* I'm still not sure myself. I really do know better.

When it comes to family media dynamics, most of us—even those who care about entertainment standards—operate as I did with this painter. Nothing is written down.

There's a better way. I'd like to suggest putting your expectations and thoughts in writing. There's something about a written agreement that can help you and your children know what's anticipated.

That's what my family did. Yes, I'm happy to say that I did a better job coming up with a written contract for my family on entertainment than I did creating something in writing for my painter.

All in the Family

Back in February 2002, the Waliszewskis were uncharacteristically glued to the tube. The reason? The Olympics. We watched Derek Parra win gold in the men's 1,500-meter speed skate. We saw Canadian ice dancers Victor Kraatz and Shae-Lynn Bourne's "planned" fall. And we caught Sarah Hughes' come-from-behind victory to clinch the gold in figure skating.

After all these hours of watching ice skating, I observed something unusual: Even my wife, Leesa, could be influenced by media.

Technically that didn't come as a surprise; I believe *everyone* can be swayed by entertainment. It's just that Leesa has been so careful about her media choices throughout our marriage.

As still another group of medalists stood during the playing of a national anthem, Leesa announced, "I want to go ice skating this weekend." It didn't take a rocket scientist to figure out where that thought had come from—especially considering it had been years since she'd glided around a rink on steel blades.

There's nothing wrong with being influenced this way, of course. If only entertainment could lead all of us to take up ice skating, cross-country skiing, or snowboarding! Many of us listen to Christian radio, read Christian books and magazines, and go to Christian Web sites because we *want* to be influenced by them. We see value in being motivated to better ourselves.

But what would have happened if my family had been watching raunchy sitcoms instead? Their unhealthy messages probably would have unraveled a lot of godly training.

That's why my family didn't stop at making a theoretical commitment to God-honoring entertainment standards. We took the additional step of adopting a family constitution for our media decisions.

How We Did It

Why a family constitution? First, my wife and I have never assumed that our two children would automatically keep practicing wise discernment once they left home. But we did believe we could help cultivate a hunger for doing things God's way. A family constitution increases one's appetite for righteousness because children see their parents spelling out and modeling its importance. Plus, there's something powerful about promising *in writing* that helps seal any decision—not to mention the accountability factor.

Assuming you're thinking, *I might like to do this,* let me walk you through my family's signing time.

Ours was not an elaborate ceremony. There was no torch-lighting, no drum roll—just a simple (and relatively brief) time together. While all of us gathered around the dinner table, I announced (Leesa knew ahead of time) that I wanted us to pledge to be Christ-honoring in our media choices. I also wanted us to seal this commitment by signing one of the "Family Covenant for God-honoring Media Choices" documents that I wrote for *Plugged In* (a "suitable-for-framing" version can be found at http://www.pluggedin.com/familyroom/articles/ 2008/afamilycovenantforgodhonoringmediachoices.aspx).

After reading the document aloud, we took turns around the table praying about our commitment. Then we signed it. It was that simple.

Looking back on this family milestone, I'm convinced it paid dividends. Not because we all got goose bumps and left with some emotional high, but because it was the right thing to do and everyone took it seriously.

Still, let me warn you: Don't wait for your children to demonstrate great enthusiasm for the idea before proceeding. Don't expect them to gush with "the wonder of it all." Chances are they won't.

Think of it not as a parting of the Red Sea, but as a loose replica of the Old Testament practice of setting up a stone memorial. After all, the power of this pledge is in the concrete evidence—the document with signatures—and the accountability it brings and the reminder as which it serves.

Though I've included in this chapter the verbiage my family used, you may want to write your own. Or you may choose to modify the one quoted here. You may want to ponder the specifics for several days and give the Lord a chance to speak to you about the matter. It will help you work through those "gray areas." It's also important that you and your spouse be of like mind as you lovingly lay down the law (after all, it will be up to *both* of you to enforce it).

Stick to your guns. Make it clear that all members of the family are subject to the newly established boundaries. This can be an especially daunting task if your spouse doesn't share your vision for entertainment purity, or you're a single parent whose child spends time with a permissive ex-spouse. In such cases ask that your rules be respected, pray for everyone involved, and when necessary seek out a neutral third party as mediator.

Whatever your parenting situation, I hope you'll actually do this—not just pass over this chapter with a, "Hmmm! That might be a good idea." When a written and signed family media constitution is in place, your kids will be much more likely to buy ice skates than the destructive lies of Hollywood.

Here's the pledge I wrote:

> As family members committed to the lordship of Jesus Christ and wanting to live out personal holiness as He commands, we pledge from this day forward to honor God in our media choices. Despite poor decisions that we may have made in the past, we desire to secure the blessings that come from obedience. Because we realize that certain types of entertainment are spiritually unhealthy, we ask the heavenly Father to guide us and strengthen us as we work to make wise choices, striving with all our effort to be imitators of God through the empowering of the Holy Spirit.
>
> Knowing that God says, "Above all else, guard your heart" (Proverbs 4:23), we pledge to guard our hearts from harmful media influences (music, films, videos, Internet, magazines, books, television, video games, etc.) that work against our faith.
>
> In the rare event that one of us feels an exception to the above should be made, we pledge to bring this issue and the reasons for it to the family to discuss and evaluate—rather than make the decision in isolation.
>
> We understand that signing this family constitution has no

field trip is canceled." She had read my note and every word of your review and taken seriously that six-year-olds did not need to see this movie. We are talking about over 300 six-year-olds. She also said that she had three other notes from parents expressing concern, but your review was all the proof she needed.

Where the Wild Things Are is just one example of how age appropriateness needs to be taken into consideration when measuring media against the family constitution. Not okay for six-year-olds, it could be fine for older children with additionally developed cognitive skills to process some of its darker elements. Stephanie realized this and stepped in, not only to protect her own daughter but 300 other first graders. I commend her—and the school administrators—for realizing that when it comes to entertainment, one "size" doesn't fit all.

Your Custom Constitution

Since the days of silent movies, the power of a motion picture with the potential to negatively affect society has not gone unnoticed. For that reason, industry pioneers drafted a self-regulatory code of ethics in 1930 that governed the content of films. These former standards of good taste, known as the Production Code, provided specific dos and don'ts concerning what could be shown in American movies, including these:

- No picture shall be produced which will lower the standards of those who see it.
- Illegal drug traffic must never be presented.
- Ministers of religion should not be used as comic characters or villains . . .
- The sanctity of marriage and the home shall be upheld.
- The words God, Lord, Jesus, and Christ are not to be used unless used reverently.[1]

There are still movies today that uphold this mostly forgotten code of yesteryear. Many don't, of course, and as a result "lower the

bearing upon our salvation (which is 100 percent dependent upon our faith in Jesus Christ as our Savior and Lord), but is an outgrowth of our desire to please God and obey Him in every area of our lives.

Family members sign below:

_____   _____
_____   _____
_____   _____
_____   _____

Date: _____

Once you, your spouse, and your children have signed your family media constitution, post it in your home where it can be readily seen. This helps everyone remember this commitment more easily.

Upholding the Constitution

If you have small children yet to request their first MP3 download or streaming video, consider yourself blessed. Your job will be easier. They can develop their entertainment habits in accordance with your constitution.

On the other hand, if you have teenagers who are already fans of questionable media content, you face an entirely different challenge.

You can start operating under the new standard "from this day forward," but you and your spouse must determine how to deal with the garbage already stashed in your child's entertainment collection. Here are some possible scenarios:

- After discovering the need for discernment through the signing ceremony, your teen may feel supernaturally convicted, voluntarily purging the junk from his music and movie library and changing his TV viewing habits.
- You can humbly accept responsibility for taking too long to "set the boundaries," and agree to replace the offending products with ones that meet the family standard. Since you're picking up the tab, you may even want to limit

"substitutes" to edifying projects by popular Christian artists—and movies, video games, and TV shows that you've
prescreened or researched online.

- After the family has measured the entertainment in question
against the family standard and weeded out everything that
flunked, you're ready to start fresh. Be diligent. Hold firm
to the new guidelines. From now on, if your preteen or teen
asks to purchase a certain media product, you can confi-
dently say, "Sure, but when you bring it home, we'll review
it together, and if it doesn't meet the written family constitution we signed, I take it and you're out the money."

No more excuses. The agreement is in writing; they can read it
for themselves. Rest assured, if your kids know it's *their* money on
the line, they'll be much more selective about which entertainers they
invite home.

Your Family Standards

A family entertainment standard is a valuable tool. But as with any
tool, using it requires *work*. Keeping that in mind, be sure not to base
your family constitution on style or ratings.

Let me be very blunt here: Rating systems are totally unreliable.
For motion pictures, a PG-13, PG, or even a G says almost nothing
about whether a film will uplift the human spirit and avoid glamorizing evil.

The same is true with television and video game ratings. Trusting a
rating system is like driving through snow with bald tires—risky! Most
of those who currently analyze media for secular outlets—be it movies,
video games, music, or television—do not approach entertainment
using a "family" filter. In fact, even if the reviewing process appears
designed to warn parents of potential pitfalls, the criteria being used
are often random and inconsistent at best.

That's why I advise families to take a skeptical approach when
a product carries a rating. Though it takes a little more research, it's
worth your time and effort to go beyond the rating and find out about

the content of a film, program, site, book, or album. Much
research can be done through reliable Web sites.

Likewise, especially when it comes to music, *style* can
deceptive. "Harder" genres can offer positive messages, wh
mellower musicians dump all sorts of lyrical sewage on their
this area, perhaps more than any other, we parents allow ou
be swayed by personal preference.

Resist that temptation. A better measure is to check ou
sages being conveyed, not the style or look of the messenge

Keep in mind, too, that some wholesome and uplif
products just aren't appropriate for all ages. Even within a f
are differences in how our children process entertainmen
be very sensitive to scenes involving peril, for instance, w
realizes that the character who's hanging on to a branch
of a cliff is going to be all right in the end.

What one child is able to view at age six may be
another until he or she is around ten. That was true in
might not seem fair, but we can't just declare that "age
a magic benchmark for all kids. You may want to add
your family media constitution that specifically addres

When the movie *Where the Wild Things Are* cam
we warned in our online review that the film would be
younger viewers. Interestingly, even *USA Today* ran
the film being inappropriate for younger children. C
Stephanie picked up on this idea when she sent the f

Thank you for your review of *Where the Wild Thing*
first grader's class was planning a field trip to see tha
After reading your review and lots of prayer, I wrot
attached your review to it. On Monday morning,
the principal of the school and told her all of my
mom and as a Christian. She was shocked and ha
ing bad about the movie. She promised to check
and send a couple of teachers to watch it. . . . [L
teachers exclaimed,] "I am so sorry, Mrs. ——.

standards of those who see [them]." How do you want your family media constitution to treat those films?

That's just one example of the decisions you'll need to make when creating your constitution. Many films, songs, video games, and other entertainment products fall into a "gray area." How will your family constitution apply?

Whatever you decide, do it only after prayer (and discussion with your spouse if you're married). All of us, if we're truly open to the Lord and seeking wisdom in this area, could benefit from closer alignment with the Creator's thoughts on this subject.

You *can* pass the "media baton" to your children without dropping it. And you can do it with less strife by agreeing on your family's standards in advance—especially if you put them in writing.

Questions that Encourage
Savvy Media Thinking

Whether you're creating a family entertainment constitution or using teachable moments to encourage your child to "think different" about media, try asking questions like these to get the discussion going.

1. What are your favorite films, television shows, video games, and albums at this point in your life? Why are they your favorites? Is it because your friends like these? If so, why are these your friends' favorites?

2. Would you describe messages of your favorites as uplifting, encouraging, and inspiring, or more of a downer? Why?

3. Do you feel your entertainment choices have any effect on how close you feel to your family, friends, or God? Why or why not?

4. Would you agree or disagree with the statement, "As a general rule, entertainment is simply harmless fun"? Explain.

5. Would you feel comfortable if Jesus sat next to you as you watched, listened to, or played those favorites? Do you think He'd have a smile on His face or would He be saddened? What do you think He would say?

6. What would happen if you imitated the lifestyles and choices of the characters in your favorite movies, television programs, and songs?

7. Do you think some individuals might act out what they've observed via their entertainment choices? Do you feel you've been influenced? Or could be?

8. Do you think our "family standard" for entertainment is fair or unfair, necessary or unnecessary? Why?

9. When you have observed entertainment that mocks, undermines, or stands opposed to the values of this family (and the Lord), how does that make you feel? Have you

laughed? Does it sadden you? How about when you hear your friends have consumed those types of media?

10. If asked by your friends to explain how to determine what entertainment is in bounds and which is out of bounds, what would you say?

eight

Frantically Asked Questions

While it's one thing to care about the impact of entertainment on our families, it's another to know what to do about it—and still another to deal with the fallout when we try.

Battles over media intake aren't inevitable, but they're all too common. When your attempts to set standards lead to icy stares or outright outbursts from your kids, what are you supposed to do?

My goals with this book are twofold. First, I want to help parents who've had teaching media discernment somewhere around Number 37 on their priority lists move it up to the Top 10. Second, I want to make this process as practical as possible.

That's why this chapter seeks to answer some "What-do-I-do-now?" questions that often arise. I hope the answers will further equip you to face the not-always-simple side of following through on the ideas in this book.

Question: My daughter's a sophomore in high school. The school district sent home a form asking for permission to let her see R rated films such as *Schindler's List* and *Saving Private Ryan* in history class. We know these films have important messages and critics loved them, but we don't want to set a precedent for letting her watch R rated films. She says if we don't let her watch, the other kids and even the teacher will see her as a "loser from a loser family." What should we do?

There may be an easy solution here that will keep everyone happy. Consider offering the school a ClearPlay video player (see Chapter 9). This device "knows" where to skip certain scenes and portions of dialogue—thanks to a flash drive containing data you download from the Internet. Then your daughter and her classmates can receive the benefit of a deeper understanding of the Holocaust without having to be exposed to the steamy sexual scene involving Liam Neeson, or the one showing Ralph Fiennes in bed with a woman, her breast exposed (*Schindler's List*). With this technology, your daughter's class also can gain a greater appreciation of those who battled on Normandy's shores without the over-the-top violence of *Saving Private Ryan.*

If the school or teacher refuses to air the edited version in class, at least your child will have the option of viewing the same movie as the rest of the class at home or in another room at school.

Question: My daughter is a strong Christian and says she's totally against the lyrics and profanity used in certain songs. But she loves rap and the beat of the music. She wants to listen to the "clean" version of the songs. I'm glad she continues to uphold some standards, but I want her to skip the whole genre. She says I'm not being fair.

First of all, I'd like to commend your daughter because she seeks to make God-honoring musical choices.

Second, a bit of background information. Because some stores refuse to stock CDs that feature parental advisory stickers, some of the most vile albums are released in two versions—one "edited" or "clean," the other not. This allows the record companies to skirt the ban and get their product into family-oriented retail outlets.

But do "clean" versions really live up to their billing? In a word, no. That's because the scouring process is usually nothing more than bleeping some of the worst obscenities, some specific references to drugs, and words like "murder," "drive-by," and "bullets."

There's no consistency in this process. It's not uncommon for "censors" to preserve a deeply objectionable theme while excluding something relatively minor. Here's an example from the "clean" version of rapper DMX's album *It's Dark and Hell Is Hot*:

> I'm coming in the house and I'm gunnin' for your spouse
> Trying to send the (bleep) back to her maker
> And if you got a daughter older than 15, I'ma [gonna] rape her.[1]

The one word edited from the original? It's used frequently as a synonym for a female dog. Meanwhile, "gunnin'" and "rape" go by in this "sanitized for your family" version.

Uniform lyric editing standards are nonexistent. Some "censors" have no problem with the b-word or the s-word. I've heard the word "marijuana" axed, while "I rap on acid [LSD]" got a pass.

The fact is that if "censors" really did their job, the clean versions of many stickered CDs would drop to about seven minutes in length—down from their original seventy. And who'd pay $12.99 for a seven-minute disc?

Record companies claim they can clean up lyrics, but they haven't earned your trust—or your daughter's. If she truly loves rap but wants to avoid twisted messages, encourage her to give Christian rappers like TobyMac, Grits, and KJ-52 a try.

Question: We're pretty strict about the movies we let our kids watch. Now that they're in middle school, they're interested in some films that contain profanity. They say the language isn't any worse than what they hear every day in the halls at school, and they're probably right. How can I say no to a few words when they'll be exposed to a flood of them anyway?

This is a toughie! Watching edited films is one way to go, though it eliminates seeing most movies in a theater.

When kids resist the idea that profanity should put a piece of entertainment off-limits, they're usually thinking along one or more of the following lines:

- If I can't go to a movie with one "bad" word, I'll never get to go to anything.
- The Bible doesn't say I can't watch a show or listen to a song with swearing in it.
- I won't start cussing just because I heard somebody else do it.

Let's consider that first thought. Does a single vulgarity disqualify a film or song? Suppose a film with a great takeaway message also contains a few mild profanities. Is that reason enough to say no to teens?

I know my answer will be controversial. But I can imagine Jesus taking His disciples to a film that has as its only objectionable element the language issue I just described. Others would disagree with me. I would change my reply if other profanities or obscenities, such as the f-bomb and misuses of Jesus' name, were part of the movie.

I still find mild profanities offensive. I believe it's best to avoid entertainment that uses it—especially for younger children. But in my opinion, most teenagers can navigate through an occasional mild profanity in entertainment without it becoming a spiritual stumbling block.

If you go the route of eliminating all films for teenagers because of mild language issues, be sure you've made it a matter of prayer and not just preference.

As for the second objection kids tend to raise, consider this excerpt from an e-mail we received from a girl named Katie: "I read your reviews and you always say something about the cuss words in music—I was wondering if you have some verses in the Bible where it says cussing is wrong."

It's a fair question. Does God specifically address or condemn vulgar speech? Actually, He does. Check out Colossians 3:8 for starters: "But now you must rid yourselves of all such things as these: anger, rage, malice, slander, and filthy language from your lips." Also, we "grieve the Holy Spirit" (Ephesians 4:30) when we violate Ephesians 4:29: "Do not let any unwholesome talk come out of your mouths." We are warned that "among you there must not be even a hint of sexual immorality, or of any kind of impurity" (Ephesians 5:3). Then

God lists a few of those things that qualify, including "obscenity, foolish talk [and] coarse joking" (Ephesians 5:4). And the Lord has plenty to say about "taming the tongue" (James 3).

But it's not enough to quote these verses. Our kids need to understand that using obscenities is a *symptom*. It's a symptom God cares about. But He's always more interested in the root problems and root solutions.

God is concerned about what comes out of our mouths because He created us in His image—and He is holy. If we belong to Christ, we've been spiritually adopted. Following a section explaining how we're "[His] sons and daughters," God tells us in 2 Corinthians 7:1 to "purify ourselves from everything that contaminates body and spirit, perfecting holiness out of reverence for God." We abstain from using obscenities and profanities not just because they "contaminate," but because as God's kids we hate to disappoint our heavenly Father.

"But," your children might protest, "that's about *using* bad language, not hearing somebody *else* use it." That brings us to the third argument—that kids won't pick up the language they encounter in shows and songs.

If we're listening to music stickered (or that should have been stickered) with a parental advisory, or watching movies or playing video games that frequently use harsh profanities, is it possible those words will cling to our minds? Personal experience alone tells me this is so.

When harsh profanities are consumed via entertainment, they're often added to our mental vocabulary. We stub our toe on the coffee table, and the next thing we know the vulgarities we've been exposed to roll off the tongue or at least in our thoughts.

As a general rule, I believe profanity mars entertainment and should give us pause before consuming media that includes it. In Chapter 9 I'll discuss technology that can edit all of it out—which in my mind is a superior option, even for the "mild" words and phrases. After you've answered the aforementioned three objections for your kids, maybe it's an option for your family, too.

Question: My son likes to argue with us that media discernment is all about censorship. He says free speech and First Amendment rights are what matter. How should we handle this ongoing debate?

In October 2009, ESPN broadcaster Bob Griese learned that in spite of concerns about free speech, there are limits to what can be said without igniting a firestorm. At the end of the Ohio State–Minnesota game, Griese made an inappropriate remark about NASCAR driver Juan Pablo Montoya, saying he was "out having a taco" when Montoya's name didn't appear among the top five drivers in the points race. Before the telecast was over, Griese apologized. ESPN issued its own apology soon thereafter. A few months later another ESPN personality, Tony Kornheiser, was temporarily suspended from his show, *Pardon the Interruption*, after making disparaging comments about *SportsCenter* anchor Hannah Storm's "horrifying" outfit.

Similar lessons have been learned by people like Senator Trent Lott, pitcher John Rocker, comedians Bill Maher and Michael Richards, the Rev. Jesse Jackson, and radio broadcasters Don Imus and Dr. Laura Schlessinger. For these offenders, few argued "free speech" in their defense. Instead, the public debate centered on the message—as it should.

For some reason, though, many media icons and entertainment role models get a free pass when it comes to what might be considered hate speech and the glamorization of illegal activity. Some receive Grammy awards or millions of dollars at the box office. Films, TV shows, and video games are also not subject to the same level of scrutiny as are some individuals who make an ill-advised or mean-spirited comment.

What if musicians, for example, faced the same scrutiny as politicians and athletes? Rapper Eminem is hardly alone in making bizarre comments, but he's been one of the most popular—having been named the Artist of the Decade by *Billboard* magazine in 2009 (80 million albums sold). No sportscaster, congressman, or federal judge ever boasted about raping his mother—which Eminem did on an album that received a Grammy award. You won't find a baseball player saying, "Follow me and do exactly what the song says: Smoke weed, take pills, drop out of school/Kill people and drink and jump behind the wheel." Eminem did that in one of his songs, "Role Model."[2]

I support Eminem's right to say what he wants to within the law. But I don't believe being a musician somehow makes him immune to analysis or criticism.

It might be helpful to let your young person know that there are at least nine forms of expression that are *not* covered by the First Amendment. For instance, it's illegal to make clear and immediate threats to national security—like disclosing information about troop movements during wartime. Libel and slander are not protected. Neither are "obscenity" and "fighting words" (like abusive language yelled by a demonstrator at a police officer). And it's unlawful to use deceptive or misleading advertisements to induce or entice minors to engage in illegal activities such as prostitution and drug or alcohol use.

Yet many of the most popular albums charting today—especially in the rap genre—"advertise" illegal substances and behaviors. And how can a musician encouraging a 10-year-old to kill his "haters" be that different from a gang leader ordering his crew to take out a rival?

The irony isn't missed by Darrell Scott, father of slain Columbine High School student Rachel Joy Scott. He once commented, "We put Charles Manson away for life. He didn't kill anyone, but he influenced his followers to do so. Eminem has more influence and more followers than Charles Manson."[3]

The issue really boils down to our children and the world they'll someday inherit. What's best for them?

Those are some of the thoughts you could share during the next round of the debate with your son. You might also ask him whether he's glad no one can legally yell "Fire!" in a crowded theater or "I've got a bomb!" on a plane. If so, shouldn't he also oppose entertainers using their platforms to lure children into criminal activity?

Question: My daughter was at a sleepover, and they were going to show a PG-13 rated movie that according to your Web site was chock-full of all sorts of steamy sexual content, innuendo,

and language—even some nudity. **She knew we don't allow that sort of thing in our home, yet she called—begging me to make an exception. She said she'd be mortified if she was the only kid who wasn't allowed to watch it. How could I say no? Or could I say yes?**

Believe me, I understand how hard it is to make decisions that seem to isolate your children or make them out to be the biggest geeks on campus. We all want our kids to be liked and admired by their peers.

That's why having rules in our homes that seem to spotlight our differentness can be a real struggle for preteens and teens. In some ways we're asking our young person to wear a sandwich board to school that reads, "Avoid me. I'm strange and I'm trying to make sure everyone knows it."

Yet, as I mentioned in an earlier chapter, self-denial is part of the Christian experience. If your child is a Christian, simply reminding him or her that God's plan often involves standing alone may make a difference.

To illustrate this important concept, take your young person to Daniel 6, the story of Daniel being tossed into the lion's den. When a decree came forth that no one could pray to anyone but King Darius for 30 days, Daniel risked slipping in popularity big-time if he chose to do anything else.

The masses went with the herd mentality. No doubt many knew it was wrong, but pretended to pray to Darius anyway so as not to rock the boat or bring undue attention to themselves. They may even have reasoned, *Hey, it's just for 30 days. Besides, I don't really mean it in my heart and that's what truly counts.*

But Daniel resisted the group-think. He decided the opinions of this peers weren't important compared to the opinions of his God. This led him to keep praying—not to Darius, and with the windows open.

The consequences were severe. Daniel was thrown into a pit of hungry lions. But the Lord had a plan: miraculous intervention. None of it could have happened without self-denial and the willingness to stand alone.

If your young person needs a more modern "lion's den" experience to serve as inspiration, here's one: Recently I received a call from a mother whose son had just returned from a sports camp. The coach told the boys he would treat them to a movie at a local theater to celebrate the camp's final night. Because the movie contained objectionable content, the boy declined the offer. As a result, the coach canceled the entire outing for the whole team.

Although somewhat humiliated, this boy knew he had done the right thing. My hat goes off to this young man for taking a stand. He hadn't tried to prevent the others from going to the movie. But he was willing to deny himself what they and the coach deemed acceptable.

In addition to telling stories like that one, you can encourage your child to resist unhealthy pressure by giving her a strong dose of affirmation whenever she *does* stand alone. There are also some things you can do to prevent situations like the one at the sleepover.

First, find out ahead of time what movie(s) are on the agenda. Most sleepovers these days seem to include at least one film. Asking beforehand helps eliminate surprises. If you discover that the film doesn't meet the family standard, offer to supply one that does. Conversations at the parental level will often nip this issue in the bud.

But what if there's a last-minute change in the movie-watching plan? Rather than calling to come home, your child could engage in some other activity in another room—reading a book, completing a homework assignment, helping the parents make refreshments, entertaining a younger family member, etc. This sends the right message to your child's friends: "I'm not judging you for watching this film. I'm just trying to guard my own heart, and I feel this film's messages aren't good for me. And I like you all so much that I'm staying around so that I can spend time with you afterward."

My daughter faced this exact scenario when she was in high school, as I mentioned earlier in this book. She spent the evening in another room with the parents. It wasn't her first choice, but it was the right one; she made the tough decision to guard her heart rather than take the easy route.

Calling you is an option, too, of course. When nothing else seems to do the trick, your child needs to know she has permission to call you anytime, day or night, to pick her up.

Question: I know we're not supposed to be hypocritical, do-what-I-say-not-what-I-do parents, but isn't it unrealistic for my wife and me to only rent movies our seven-year-old son could watch? How are we ever going to see anything more intense than *Ice Age*?

One of my favorite films to date is *The Passion of the Christ*. I was moved by this film's portrayal of Christ's sacrifice for me. Still, the scenes of Jesus' brutal torture and crucifixion are without question extremely graphic and tremendously harsh to witness.

This film is so gripping and persuasive that I believe every person on the planet should watch it at least once. But not until about age 12 or 13. This most certainly is not a film for your seven-year-old. Or nine-year-old.

Is it wrong to watch it and inform your son that he'll need to wait until he's a bit older to see it? No.

You can explain why by saying something like this: "Jesus was crucified for our sins. This movie shows that in a way that could be too upsetting for kids. I want you to see this film, too, someday. But not just yet. In the meantime, let's read again what the Bible says happened on that day."

As for all those other films you'd like to watch but know they aren't age-appropriate for your son, here's a question to ask yourself: *Would I want my child to see this film when he's older?* If the honest answer is yes, there's probably no hypocrisy involved. If it's no, make another choice.

You're right to be concerned about practicing what you preach. If there's one aspect of parenting that seems to have the greatest lasting negative impact, it's when our kids see us acting in a hypocritical way. It tends to breed rebellion.

Question: My husband and I don't rent anything raunchy, but some of the DVDs we watch in our bedroom have some minor

inappropriate content we don't want our 12-year-old daughter to see or hear. We lock the door during these movies, but sometimes wonder if she's listening. Are we doing the wrong thing?

Once again, I suggest watching films through a ClearPlay machine (see Chapter 9) to edit out inappropriate content. Rarely do these edits mar the film-watching experience. In fact, in my opinion, the edits enhance the viewing.

Question: It seems like whenever we rent or download a movie, my teenagers and I get into an argument. They gravitate toward direct-to-video PG-13 horror movies and comedies I've never heard of, the kind that never get reviewed anywhere but look suspect. They're always willing to take a chance. Of course, I'm not. I don't want to watch these things first in order to decide whether they're okay. How can we avoid these battles?

First, there's a bigger issue here than whether or not to watch direct-to-DVD movies. It's the tendency in your teens to want films that look suspect just from the titles and artwork on the packaging. To overcome this tendency, other principles I've highlighted must come into play first: A hatred of evil, a desire to honor the Lord with all decisions including media ones, an understanding of the influence of entertainment, and an acknowledgment that biblical principles should guide wise entertainment choices.

If your teens don't grasp those concepts, you'll want to work on that. If they do, the question highlights what we've all discovered: Choosing a film can be extremely difficult. I suggest always making these decisions ahead of time. Go online. Read the comments of a film-review Web site you can trust (like pluggedin.com). Decide what you're going to rent *before* you get to the store or video streaming site or vending machine. Come prepared with two choices in case your top pick isn't available.

One more suggestion: Try keeping a running list of films you're interested in, based on ongoing research you and your kids have been doing together. Discuss the reviews you read; make this an opportunity to deepen your relationship, not just to debate. Instead of relying on memory or packaging, consult the list when it's time to make a rental or downloading decision.

Question: My son is in the sixth grade. The other day, when I was looking for a school form to sign, I discovered two R rated "teen sex comedy" DVDs in his backpack. When I asked him about them, he said his friend Ray loaned them to him. In addition to not wanting my son to watch this stuff, I doubt Ray's parents would be happy about this. My son asked me not to tell them about it. I feel like I should, but know my son would feel betrayed and embarrassed. What should I do?

It's a good thing you discovered these DVDs. You didn't mention whether or not your son had already viewed one or both of them, but let's assume he hasn't. It's very likely Ray has. Having your son hang out with a "friend" who consumes soft-core porn can only be a problem.

What should you do? Your son's potential embarrassment if you speak to Ray's parents is a minor concern when compared to the alternative: being exposed to sexual content that could ultimately lead to a fascination with pornography. Putting a stop to this immediately is crucial. To do this, you'll need the help of Ray's parents; they can't help if they don't know what's going on. If they *do* know, you won't be making Ray's situation worse by telling them.

Think of it this way. What if the situation were reversed? Wouldn't you want Ray's parents to inform you?

Now, you don't want to be accusatory when you broach this subject with them. You could start by saying something like, "We knew you'd probably want to know about a discovery we made today." Next, suggest that both sets of parents and both boys get together for a serious discussion.

Do what you can to obey Romans 12:18, which says, "If it is possible, as far as it depends on you, live at peace with everyone." But be willing to put your foot down about your son hanging out with Ray if you feel there's no remorse or repentance from him when he's confronted with the truth.

Question: If I ask, my daughter always tells me what movie she and her friends are going to at the Cineplex. The problem is that she doesn't always tell me the truth. Another parent saw her sneaking into a different movie, one she knew I wouldn't approve. I can't be there to keep her in the "right" theater, so what can I do?

Again, there are bigger issues here than media discernment—issues such as honesty, trust, and handling peer pressure.

So I'll rephrase the question: When it's so easy to buy a ticket for a decent movie but sneak into something offensive, how can I be confident my child isn't taking advantage of this situation at the Cineplex?

I would suggest always having a follow-up conversation with your child about the movies he or she views. Read reviews ahead of time, of course. When your child returns, ask questions along these lines: "Tell me about this movie. What was its most redeeming message? If your little sister wanted to go see it, what would you say? Why would you recommend this film to your other friends, or would you?"

By asking probing questions that can't be answered with a simple yes or no, you'll get a feel for whether your child attended the approved movie. You'll also help build in her the discernment muscles every filmgoer needs.

Keep in mind, however, that theaters aren't the only place our children can watch problematic movies. Writer and mother Liz Perle, in her article "Sneaking into R-Rated Movies (Without Leaving Home)," wrote this:

> I clearly recall telling my then 13-year-old son that the movie
> *Superbad* was a total non-starter for him. [Since it was] full of
> underage drinking, I didn't want him to think getting plastered
> was hilarious. So he didn't go sneak into the theater with his
> friends. But a week later, he was quoting movie dialogue. He
> didn't need to see the movie. He simply went online and watched
> the trailers. Then he went on to YouTube for more. Finally, he
> illegally downloaded a pirated user-posted copy by using an open
> source file-sharing application called BitTorrent. A total wipeout.
> Not only had he seen the movie, but he'd also broken the law.

As if that wasn't enough, he'd also downloaded spyware malware onto his new(ish) computer. Which slowed to a crawl within a week.[4]

Question: Our family vacations usually involve long-distance driving. Our kids get restless, and my husband wants our next vehicle to have a DVD player in it. I think it's a waste of money, and would rather have the kids play the license plate game and look at the scenery. My husband insists the world has changed, and I'd better get used to it. Who's right?

In my opinion, you're both right. Your children should play car games and they should also be enjoying the scenery.

But let's say you're driving through eastern Kansas (sorry, Kansans!). After "enjoying" the 58th wheat field and their fifth round of car bingo, is there really any problem with watching a 90-minute, positive-themed movie? I think not!

In fact, maybe it should be your turn to drive. Let your husband squeeze into that middle backseat, where he can join your kids for some family-friendly DVD viewing.

I realize, of course, that there are good reasons not to spend money on luxuries. You and your husband need to prayerfully consider that issue. But a DVD player probably won't destroy your children's character. Perhaps a compromise would be to rent or borrow a portable DVD player for one trip and see how it works out.

Question: When our kids were very young, we got rid of our TV. That's helped us avoid some problems, but has led to others. Right now the problem is that the kids are assigned to watch certain shows (a presidential speech, a documentary) for school. We're afraid that if we get a TV for that purpose, we'll waste all kinds of time watching junk. What can we do?

You have every reason to be concerned about today's television viewing. Instead of taking an all-or-nothing approach, though, you might consider having a TV that's hooked up to a DVR (a digital video recorder that can record programming, pause live television, and advance through commercials) or VCR (yes, the old-fashioned video-cassette recorder). Then you can record that presidential speech, Civil War documentary, or congressional hearing.

A recording device won't prevent TV-watching for non-educational purposes, of course. I don't find that to be a problem. Just be careful about what your family views. I'm fine with allowing 30 minutes—even an hour—of positive or neutral television per day. Other parents may prefer different limits. Recording in advance what you'll watch may help to enforce those limits as you *choose* programs rather than staring at whatever happens to be on. And advancing past commercials via a DVR or VCR not only saves time (about eight minutes every half hour) but prevents exposure to ads that push the envelope.

By owning a TV set and using it responsibly, you can help develop discernment skills that will last long after your kids leave home. They'll be less likely to tell themselves, "Wait 'til I'm out of this place. Not only will I own a TV, but I'll watch whatever I want, whenever I want." An attitude like that is, of course, counter to what you're trying to foster in their hearts.

Question: My eight-year-old son tends to get nightmares when he watches even a mildly scary TV show, but he's drawn to them anyway. When he asks to watch these shows, he always says he won't have a bad dream this time. If I say no, he says I should believe him. When can I start saying yes?

I assume we're not talking here about programs that could be called horror, "slasher," or occultic; I'm not into that for any age group, and I don't think God is, either. If the problem truly is your son's sensitivity, it might be wise to wait until he turns 10, 11, or 12 to try again with "mildly scary" entertainment. You're the best one to determine age appropriateness.

Letting your son know that these shows aren't out of the question forever—just until he's a bit older—should go a long way in keeping this "no" from becoming an ongoing battle.

As for dealing in the meantime with your son's tendency toward nightmares, here's what psychologist Dr. Bill Maier had to say on a

Focus on the Family broadcast about helping a child with bad dreams and nighttime fears:

> . . . It's fairly common for young children to experience bedtime fears. Their little imaginations are developing like wildfire and they don't have the ability to distinguish fantasy from reality. In their minds, there really *is* a monster in the closet or under the bed. . . .
>
> [If] he has a night light in his room . . . make sure it doesn't cast any scary shadows on the wall. That occurred with our son, and we solved the problem by simply moving the night light to a different outlet. You could also pick out a stuffed animal that can be his special "bedtime buddy," providing him with comfort when you're not there. You might also buy an inexpensive CD player for his room and let him listen to some comforting [tunes] or kids' worship songs just before he falls asleep.
>
> Most importantly, remind him that God loves him and that He promises us He will always be with us and take care of us. Continue to pray with him each night when you tuck him in, and teach him to pray simple prayers if he wakes up in the night, asking God to help him to not be afraid.[5]

Question: Some families we know seem to have a TV in every room, but we've only got one—and don't want another. The problem is that we can't agree on what shows to watch. We know we can watch one while recording another, but sometimes that leaves a third person out in the cold. At other times, someone wants to watch a recorded program when someone else is watching live. How can everybody get a turn?

I commend you for having a single television set in your home. As you know, that's pretty atypical these days. When you own only one TV, it's much easier to regulate. It also keeps the tube out of your children's bedrooms where, in my opinion, it doesn't belong.

As for everyone getting a turn, try limiting TV viewing to 30 minutes or an hour per day and using a DVR or VCR to record programming. Even if your family is fairly large, you should have greater success in making sure everyone gets to watch his or her favorite show. On occasions when this doesn't work, encourage family members to negotiate—perhaps trading TV time or offering to do extra chores in return for tube access.

I'm assuming you don't have a computer and Internet connection that would allow you to watch archived TV shows online at network and other Web sites such as hulu.com or TvLand.com; if you do, there's another source (as long as you monitor the time spent and programs viewed).

Question: I read that some group of doctors advised that babies and toddlers shouldn't watch television. Then I saw that those "baby genius" videos don't work. But my wife is home with the kids all day, and if she never plunked the kids in front of a TV she'd go nuts. Is it really hurting them to give her a break?

The general consensus these days among researchers is that children should not be exposed to *any* television for the first two years of development. I know it's hard, but you and your wife need to resist the urge to occupy the kids with tube time during these early formative years.

Perhaps it will help to keep in mind that for most of mankind's history, the TV set wasn't even an option and somehow parents survived. (Okay, maybe that won't help!) Arranging play dates and babysitting co-ops with other parents might be even more helpful when you and your wife need a break.

During toddlerhood, introducing some positive television—a maximum of 30 minutes per day—is fine. Not only will it give you a bit of relief (especially after not using the TV for two years or so); it can expose your children to some of the more constructive, Christian-themed video content available.

Question: My kids are five and seven. We try to monitor what they watch on TV, but sometimes in the middle of an acceptable show they're bombarded by commercials we don't want them to see—either because of the product or the way it's being pitched. If

we're there and we turn the TV off during the ad, it just feeds their curiosity and leads to cries of, "Turn it back on!" How can we cut out these commercials?

As I've mentioned, I'm a firm believer in the DVR. Since the invention of the TV there's never been a device that can help us so much with ads.

And we do need help. We're all busy people, so why waste time watching commercials? Furthermore, even highly offensive ads can air during some "family friendly" shows or sporting events. Who needs that?

I suggest using a DVR or VCR to record *everything* your children might watch. Then train them—even at ages five to seven—to fast-forward through the commercials. Show them how to do it. It won't take them long to catch on.

Not only will your family members steer clear of sleazy ads; they'll also turn a 30-minute viewing into a 22-minute endeavor. Who couldn't use the extra eight minutes?

Question: Recently we were stopped at a red light and the person in the car next to us was playing his music very loud. In a matter of just a few seconds, our young children were exposed to awful language and thematic material (although I don't think they caught the themes). What should we do when our kids are "accidentally" pelted with offensive content?

If you're like me, you want to scream, "Plug your ears, kids! Cover your eyes!" But more often than not, these incidents happen too fast and are too much out of our control.

I hope they'll be rare for you. But when they occur, I'd encourage you to turn them into teachable moments.

I don't want to mislead you into thinking that when my kids were growing up we had this down to a science; we didn't. But we did make it a point to use situations like these to reinforce principles of discernment that we were already talking about at home.

When Kelsey was nine and Trevor six, for example, we got away for a few days of snow skiing. After an afternoon of schussing, falling, and sunburning, we headed to a nearby pizza restaurant. As our meal arrived, someone dropped a pocketful of quarters in the jukebox. The first song that blared through the establishment was a song I found problematic, due to its very nihilistic worldview.

I looked across the table at Leesa. She rolled her eyes as if to say, "What's this trash we're stuck listening to?"

We felt stymied. But I resisted the urge to yell, "Okay, kids, grab the pizza and let's head to the car right now!" I used this teachable moment to explain (again) that some forms of entertainment just aren't healthy for our ears and hearts. "Who needs to hear that the world is all bad and that there's no hope?" I asked. This was a concept my children—even at that young age—could understand.

Not long after that experience, Kelsey and I were in the car together. I'd been channel surfing on the radio, and was tuned to a country station. I'm usually good about changing the dial when I need to, but I got distracted. "Daddy," Kelsey asked, "is that a good song?" It wasn't. I turned it off, a bit embarrassed—but pleased that Kelsey had recognized the song's weaknesses on her own.

After another incident like the one at the pizza parlor, I asked Trevor what he'd learned. His reply was priceless: "It was bad music."

"What is bad music?" I asked.

"Music about killing people," my daughter replied. On another occasion I'd heard her define it as "music with bad words."

As my children got older, we discussed other problematic elements—including sexual issues. But at that point in their lives, "killing people" and "bad words" were things they understood.

Will your kids be blindsided by unwelcome "entertainment" at stoplights, restaurants, and elsewhere? You can count on it. But using these times as teachable moments will produce a lifetime of positive fruit. You can count on that, too.

Question: Our kids tend to watch pretty innocent stuff on TV, but they spend way too much time on it. They never go outside. They've managed not to get obese or anything, but it bothers me that they're missing so many other things life has to offer. If I try

to get them off the couch, they complain their way through the activity and can't wait to get back to the screen. How can I change this pattern?

First, consider yourself fortunate that your children's couch-potato ways haven't resulted in excessive weight gain. Of 173 analyzed studies related to media, a full 80 percent indicated one or more adverse correlations (including obesity) when it comes to kids' media exposure.[6]

What's more, children who develop a habit of excessive TV viewing are likely to carry that habit into adulthood—where those who watch more than four hours of television per day are 80 percent more likely to die of cardiovascular disease than those who watch less than two hours.[7]

You're the parent; you set the rules. It's great that you see your children's mistakes, but you must put your foot down and take charge.

I suggest adopting a reward system for TV viewing. For every 15 minutes of physically active play, exercise, or sports, offer compensation—for instance, a gold star or points (remember, points are free; why offer a single point when you can offer 1,000 or more?). Allow kids to redeem these stars or points for certain amounts of TV viewing—for example, four stars or 4,000 points (an hour's worth of exercise) for 30 minutes of television.

No exercise means no TV. Be firm. You'll be amazed how physically active your children will become in a very short while!

Question: My kid is always listening to his iPod, but I have no idea what he's listening to. How can I monitor what he's hearing? Should I even try?

I'm big on entering your kid's entertainment world. So, yes, you should monitor his musical choices. But don't jump to being a snoop (though there's a place for that in some situations).

Begin by asking your child what he's listening to. If it's a band you've never heard of, ask about the genre and what the songs tend to be about. Google the band and its song lyrics. Then you can knowingly discuss what you liked and why. If you find something that doesn't meet the family standard, you'll soon learn that as well.

If your child uses iTunes, log on. In the version that's current at this writing, you'll find the word "Library" in the upper left part of the home page after clicking on "File." Click on "Library" and it'll display all the songs on your son's iPod.

But don't use this method exclusively. If your child wants to keep you in the dark, there are ways to beat the system. After he downloads music to his iPod, he can simply delete all files on his iTunes account. This method will keep him from revisiting those musical selections in the future, but it prevents your knowing what he downloaded—if that's his intent.

The most constructive way to stay abreast of your son's musical choices is to ask him. The most reliable may be to examine the iPod itself. The list of songs, artists, videos, podcasts, and even photos (if any) will be stored there. (Note: If your child owns a different brand of MP3 player, refer to the instructions for that device.)

Question: A couple of families at church have found out that I let my son listen to rap music—not all of it, but some. They can't believe I'm so "permissive" and are practically shunning me. They say I'm making it harder for them to maintain their families' standards when their kids can say, "But So-and-so gets to listen." Is it up to me to keep the peace here?

There's nothing inherently wrong with rap music. At this writing, however, there's very little mainstream rap that's positive and uplifting. The choices are pretty much Christian rap or some very disturbing secular stuff.

If it's the top-charting rap music that you're allowing your son to listen to, let me ask you: Where do you draw the line? Is it okay for your child to listen to a track that advocates one drive-by shooting, but not two? Okay to let him listen to a track that glamorizes marijuana, but not cocaine? To me, that's splitting hairs.

If you're letting your son consume problematic rap music, I'd have to agree with the families who believe you're making it harder for them to construct healthy boundaries. In my experience, allowing your son to step over the line now will encourage him to take even further liberties down the road. Why go there? I'd suggest that you disallow the junk and allow only the wholesome. And be sure to let these parents know about your change of heart.

If, however, you've found a positive or neutral mainstream rap song or two, you've made a rare discovery. Go ahead and consent to them. Just make sure the parents who find you too "permissive" understand your reasons.

As a rule, though, I hope you'll let these dads and moms know you're in their camp. And that you, too, will work diligently to uphold safeguards that will be productive in the long run. It may not take a village to raise a child, but it sure doesn't hurt when the villagers are on the same page.

Question: I just discovered that my daughter has a whole collection of CDs, all of which are labeled with a parental advisory. I'd like to torch 'em in the backyard, or at least run over them with my pickup. But that probably won't improve our relationship. How can I get this awful music out of my daughter's life without her wanting me out of hers?

If you've never really talked with your daughter about what it means to make healthy, God-honoring entertainment choices, torching the CDs is not your best course of action. Instead, I'd suggest a buy-back policy.

Find out how many discs she owns. Pay her an acceptable amount for each; offering the price for which your local pawn shop retails them would be fair. When she sees you're not coming into her room with a sledgehammer and a garbage can, she'll more readily understand that you have her best interest at heart.

Be sure to talk about what it means to own permissible entertainment products. Make that discussion part of writing a family media constitution (see Chapter 7). Let her know if she's ever in doubt about what's allowed, she can ask you.

Also make sure that she realizes the buyback policy is only in place until your family constitution is complete. From then on, if she violates the family standard, you'll have the option of laying the CDs out behind the tires of your pickup.

Question: I've tried to get my teens to listen to contemporary Christian music instead of their favorite bands, but they just don't like it. Maybe it's too much like church. Anyway, if I can't get them to switch, should I work toward getting them to quit listening completely?

I'm a big believer in Christian music. I've found encouragement in the messages, which often reinforce biblical truth. Through worship tunes, I've found a greater sense of intimacy with the Lord.

I am not, however, one who believes secular tunes are inherently of the devil. How many times have you sung "Happy Birthday"? Not quite a Christian song, is it?

As I've already noted, I think there are three types of entertainment: positive, neutral, and negative. If your kids are listening to the first two, consider yourself fortunate. Let them listen!

Still, it doesn't hurt to encourage them to become more knowledgeable about contemporary Christian music (CCM). Getting them to switch to CCM, or at least more of it than they're currently listening to, may be as simple as getting them past a common misconception.

Over the years, countless teens have told me they believe the quality of Christian music just isn't up to that of mainstream music. My ears tell me otherwise. In spite of my protests, these teens dig in their heels, certain they can detect some type of CCM audio-deficiency.

A few years ago I decided to get to the bottom of this debate by interviewing three well-respected music producers, all of whom have lent their talents to both top-name secular and CCM albums. I asked Michael Omartian, David Kershenbaum, and Rick Will if they felt Christian music was artistically inferior to what's charting in the mainstream.

Omartian, whose résumé includes work for Whitney Houston, Christopher Cross, Amy Grant, and 4Him, said, "There might have been a time when the argument [that CCM is second-rate] could be made." However, he believes those days are long gone.

As Omartian sees it, teens asserting mainstream music's preeminence are putting up a smoke screen to cover a deeper issue. "If you're in a room with a bunch of nonbelievers and someone turns on a Christian tune, are you thinking about it from the standpoint, 'Am I embarrassed by the message?' The music could be fantastic but the minute the word 'Jesus' comes on, are you ashamed of that or are you proud of that?"

Fair enough. But what about the perception that CCM artists are frustrated also-rans who didn't have the ability to make it in the "big leagues"? "There are actually a lot of Christian artists who are more talented than the pop artists," said Rick Will, who's shared studios with Matchbox 20 and No Doubt—as well as Charlie Peacock and CeCe Winans. "They are more educated musically. They are better rounded—not getting caught up in trying to be famous and all the things that go with that."

I couldn't help but ask how CCM can possibly keep pace with mainstream releases whose production budgets are seemingly endless. Will explained, "There are ways to make great records cheaply. Our mixing time might be a percentage less than we would spend on an L.A. pop record, but I really don't think that has affected the work. [With today's digital equipment], people can record at home and it can sound terrific."

According to Omartian, it's a much more level playing field than one might think. "It really comes down to using the equipment or using whatever you have and the ideas and creativity," he said. "I did a record recently that was the cheapest two-song recording I've ever made, and it happens to contain two of my favorite tracks I've ever done."

Kershenbaum, a 20-year veteran with more than 40 gold and platinum records to his credit (by artists including Tracy Chapman, Bryan Adams, Tori Amos, Blessid Union of Souls, and Kim Hill) added, "As long as one is prepared, and you go in the studio knowing exactly what you want to do, the musicians are quick enough and good enough to easily record within budget constraints."

Will agreed that it doesn't take a fortune to make a first-class record if the other elements are in place: "I think when you have great songs, like Margaret Becker's *Soul* CD, you can record on your dictaphone and it will happen. If the song is amazing, the process and recording are secondary. That's why there's great Christian records all over the place. It's about the song first and the honesty of it."

I hope you'll share the comments of these three gifted gentlemen with your kids, especially if your teens have relegated CCM to back-of-the-bus status. It would be a shame for them to miss some amazing music that could enrich their lives.

Question: Why do kids have to play their music so loud? Is it because their iPods are making them deaf? If I ask my kids to turn down their music, they gripe. If I ask them to use headphones or earbuds, they do that—but they don't turn down the volume. So they probably are going deaf. I'm sure when they go to concerts, they're getting as close to the speakers as possible. I can't follow them around to make sure the sound is turned down or that they're putting their fingers in their ears when necessary. How can I protect their hearing?

I can sure relate to this question! Recently my wife and I attended a concert at Denver's Pepsi Center. Although the two headliners occasionally played acoustic numbers, a lot of the tunes were extremely loud, electric guitar-driven songs. There were times I resorted to stuffing my ears with tissue. At one point Leesa and I walked outside the main auditorium to get some relief. Even the day after the concert, she complained that her ears were ringing.

I need to confess something here. I haven't been very good to my ears. As an adolescent, I attended several very loud concerts—and I can't recall a single time I walked out or used earplugs or tissue. I may have occasionally put my fingers in my ears, but that was probably rare. As a result, I have some hearing loss to this day. I'm pretty certain that I have no one to blame but myself.

As for iPods, I often listen to music or podcasts through headphones—especially when I exercise. Because I've done it wrong for so many years, I'm now keenly aware of what constitutes a safe volume level. I believe this awareness came mostly from taking a hearing test and seeing the results graphed on paper. As I observed how my hearing differed from what was considered normal, it finally dawned on me that I needed to make some changes.

According to the *Journal of the American Medical Association,* approximately one in five American teenagers suffers some type of hearing loss. An Australian study, meanwhile, found a link between hearing loss and the use of MP3 players—a 70 percent increased risk. And a study of New York college students found that more than half listened to their portable music players above recommended volume levels.[8]

As for protecting your children's hearing, I suggest getting their ears tested. Keep the results in a file. A couple of years from now, get them retested.

Have a professional interpret the two tests. Has there been a significant change?

While you're getting your children's hearing tested, engage the audiologist with questions. What has he or she observed about MP3 players? Concerts? What advice would this professional give?

You may want to call ahead and give the audiologist a heads-up on what you intend to ask, and why. We all know there are times when our children will take advice better from others; I suggest letting this be one of those times.

Question: I caught my daughter downloading some pirated music. She thinks nobody gets hurt and that she can't afford to buy CDs from those "humongous wealthy record companies." How can I get her to see that what she's doing is wrong?

Somehow the Internet's ease of accessibility has lulled many into thinking that there's a giant pot of free music out there for the taking. I encourage kids to compare illegally downloaded music to something more concrete: shoplifting.

Ask your daughter this question: What would you think about a person who went into Best Buy or Target with baggy clothes and lots of pockets for the purpose of loading up with all the CDs he or she could hide, and sneaking out of the store? Chances are your child will say something like, "Oh, that would be stealing! That would be wrong!"

Once you make that connection, it's not hard to point out that just because something is available online and doesn't come in a jewel case, it's still theft. Your daughter may not need to be reminded that God was the first to declare that taking something that doesn't belong to her is wrong. But just in case, it's His eighth commandment.

As for your daughter's attempt to justify her actions by saying the record companies have deep pockets, remind her that God's view of stealing has nothing to do with the financial assets of the victim. Stealing is stealing, period!

In case she's not fully convinced, ask her how she'd feel about this scenario: She goes to the bank to withdraw $100 from her account to do some Christmas shopping. As she counts the bills and walks outside, a homeless man snatches the money from her hand and runs off. But he shouts over his shoulder, "I'm only taking your money because you're wealthier than I am—I don't even *have* a bank account."

How would she feel? Would his lack of resources make her think, *Well, I'm okay with the fact that he stole my money because he has less than I do*? Probably not. Choosing to donate money to the man would be one thing; having it stolen from you would be another.

Furthermore, "humongous wealthy record companies" aren't the only ones who suffer when music is pirated. What about the musicians themselves, many of whom (apart from the superstars) increasingly struggle to make a living from their art?

Don't Give Up

There's no doubt about it: Practicing media discernment isn't always simple or easy, and it can increase family friction—at least temporarily. But as I hope my suggestions in this chapter have shown, it doesn't have to turn your home into a firing range or a concentration camp.

There's always a solution, perfect or not, as long as you and your child keep the lines of communication open.

Here's how authors Joe White and Lissa Johnson put it:

> Want to close the gap between you and your [child]?
>
> Communicating is the key to every relationship, even yours.
>
> No matter where you find yourself on the levels of intimacy, you can build trust between the two of you. You can confront without disconnecting, and in time the confrontations can become fewer and further between. As one teen told us, "[My parents and I] worked on building our communication skills. Now there's less anger and tension between us."
>
> It's never too late to start communicating with your [child].
>
> And it's always too soon to quit trying.[9]

part three

Keeping
the Peace
and Passing
It On

nine

Getting Technology on Your Side

Before my daughter was married, we took one last family-only vacation. While we were at dinner one evening, the restaurant's background music featured classic tunes from the '60s and '70s. I challenged my family to a game of "Name that Artist."

Okay, it wasn't a fair competition since the music was mostly unfamiliar to my children—and my wife never did care much for the hits of "our" generation. But even I was stumped on one song. It sounded familiar, but I couldn't come up with the band's name. That's when my son, Trevor, pulled out his cell phone; a few clicks later, he proudly announced the artist.

How? His mobile phone has an application that can identify songs and the people who recorded them. Go figure!

Computer scientist Alan Kay once said, "Technology is anything that was invented after you were born."[1] In my case, that cell phone app certainly applies. Still, while it's nearly impossible to keep on top of *all* the latest, fastest, and coolest technological advances, most parents are no longer totally in the dark. The "technology gap" has shrunk considerably in the last few years to the point where many mothers and fathers regularly "text" their kids—some even while they're in the same house! (I don't recommend this.) They tweet the latest "newsworthy" event and keep up with their kids' peers by "friending" them on Facebook.

So, if the tech divide has been bridged, what's the great challenge?

Perhaps it's arguing over how much time your preteen spends on social networking sites like Facebook, or on YouTube. Maybe it's your daughter's desire to have unlimited texting on the cell phone or a tendency to walk around the house wearing earbuds, listening to countless hours of music on her MP3 player. Maybe it's whether your son should compete against video gamers across the globe while Skyping his international opponents.

Most likely your young person will be online sometime today. With wireless Internet and phones that double as computers, will he or she be exposed to harmful influences—right under your nose?

What You Don't Know Can Hurt Your Kids

Even though the "technology gap" isn't what it once was, it would be naïve to say it's a non-issue. Depending upon where you are on the technology curve, it's still possible that your child's expertise with a certain product, software, or device puts him or her at risk—while you remain unaware. If not, the *next* hot product may become that Trojan horse.

Because technology is moving at a breakneck pace, evaluating the implications of new devices and tools could be a full-time job. What's more, products released to rave reviews just a few years ago (and that we finally understand) now gather dust on the shelves of Goodwill stores.

Fortunately, we don't all have to become tech geeks. We just need to know what our own children are into—and become familiar with the benefits, pitfalls, and safeguards technology provides. But no matter where you are on the gizmo-knowledge curve, protecting your kids from the negative aspects of technology requires active parental involvement.

What to Know #1: How Much Your Child Is Using Technology
Many parents are in the dark when it comes to the amount of time their kids spend on screens and smartphones. Psychologist Dr. Archibald Hart tells this story in his book *Sleep, It Does a Family Good*:

The call from Todd's school counselor came out of the blue. Fortunately Melissa, mother of 15-year-old Todd, was at home that morning. She wasn't feeling well and had taken the day off to rest.

"Mrs. Andrews, I am sorry to have to call you at home, but there is a problem with Todd's schoolwork that I need to talk to you about. When can we meet?"

Melissa had no idea that there was anything amiss. She called her husband, Jim, at work. "There's a problem with Todd at school, and the counselor wants to talk to us. . . . No, I have no idea what it's about; just tell me when you can be available so we can go see the counselor."

The counselor came right to the point. "I've received several reports from Todd's teachers that he falls asleep at his desk on a regular basis. They've tried chiding him, but it doesn't seem to be getting better. You need to look into the problem. Maybe he has a sleep disorder," the counselor suggested.

Jim and Melissa confronted Todd as soon as he came home from school. "It's no big deal. It's only happened a couple of times," he replied, dismissing the issue. But Melissa and Jim insisted on getting some help and came to my office for counseling.

At first, I met with only Jim and Melissa. I suggested they do a sleep assessment for Todd and gave them some tests to fill out, not unlike the assessment forms I'll present later. "And," I said, "please check Todd's cell phone records and see how often he uses his phone at night."

"Cell phone records?" Both seemed taken aback.

"Yes," I said, "cell phone records. Something must be keeping him awake until very late if you are sending him to bed at a reasonable hour. Trust me."

We soon found out that Todd had been text-messaging his friends until the early hours of the morning. He did it in the dark, under the covers, so his parents wouldn't know. It appeared that he was falling asleep around three o'clock most mornings, presumably from sheer exhaustion. He'd have kept going till sunrise otherwise. Todd did not have a sleep disorder—only lax family supervision! Welcome to the average American family.[2]

Seventeen-year-old Mikaela Espinoza confirms how widespread the problem is: "Whenever I'd hear my phone ring, I would, like, wake up and answer it. I think a whole bunch of kids text all night long."

Mikaela's doctor determined that her migraines were caused by too little sleep due to excessive texting. "Before technology, we went to sleep when the sun went down," says Dr. Myrza Perez, a specialist in sleep disorders. "Now, with all these distractions, teenagers alone in their rooms stay up to extremely late hours on their cell phones and computers. Their parents have no idea."[3]

Margie Ryerson, a California therapist, describes the habit as the "CNN Syndrome": Some kids crave round-the-clock updates on what their friends are doing, wearing, even eating.[4]

According to Maggie Jackson, author of *Distracted: The Erosion of Attention and the Coming Dark Age*, "[Adolescents live in] an institutionalized culture of interruption, where our time and attention is being fragmented by a never-ending stream of phone calls, e-mails, instant messages, text messages and tweets."[5]

Never before has there been such a constant invasion of *stuff* coming at our kids left and right. Failure to monitor at least a percentage of these interruptions is, I believe, ill-advised.

So is ignoring the possibility that our kids may be addicted to technology. A British study suggests that "tech addiction" is a growing problem among teenagers. About 63 percent of the 11- to 18-year-olds polled said they felt addicted to the Internet; more than half said they felt addicted to their cell phones.[6] One high school freshman from Hackensack, New Jersey, summed up what many teenagers feel about their mobile phones when she told CBS, "When I don't have my phone, I feel like I'm not going to make it through my day."[7]

Many young people also seem overly attached to Facebook, Twitter, and other social networking sites. The Nielsen Company, looking at global Internet use in 2010, found that Facebook users spent an average of more than 5.5 hours on the site per month—up from 2 hours, 10 minutes spent there just two years before. In the U.S. alone, time spent on Facebook surged by 200 percent between 2009 and 2010, and time spent on Twitter shot up 368 percent.[8] To be fair, this fascination with social networking is not limited to teenagers and pre-teens. One recent study of adult women ages 18 to 34 found that one-third check Facebook before they use the bathroom in the morning![9]

And speaking of tech addiction, let's not forget video games. From June 2008 to June 2009, the amount of time the average console video gamer spent playing each month jumped 21 percent to 12.8 hours, according to Nielsen Media Research.[10] Video game designer Paul Bertone, Jr., of Microsoft's Bungle Studios, speaking before the launch of *Halo 3*, made this claim: "We do a lot of testing to make sure that it's easy to pick up, easy to play, and hopefully, easy to get addicted to."[11]

I realize moms and dads are not omniscient, nor omnipresent. But a lot of the problem can be solved by simply asking questions and becoming familiar with the devices your child uses to obtain information, network with friends, and consume entertainment. I'd venture to say that Todd's and Mikaela's parents could have headed off those sleep and migraine problems by simply taking a closer look at their families' mobile phone bills.

But isn't that being a *snoop?* I don't believe so! That's called wise parenting—which brings us to the next point.

What to Know #2: What Your Child Is Doing with Technology

I told my children up front that e-mails, instant messaging, and Internet history were open to other family members. They could read mine; I could read theirs. I could check the sites they visited, and they were welcome to see where I'd been.

When my children lived under my roof, I regularly visited their social networking sites (and still do, for different reasons). I not only wanted to see how my kids expressed themselves, but frequently clicked on their friends' sites to check out photos they posted, polls they answered, and questionnaires they'd filled out.

Some parents might be reluctant to try this, believing it to be an unhealthy invasion of privacy. But consider this: In 2008, 22 percent of managers checked job applicants' social networking profiles before hiring. A year later, that jumped to 38 percent.[12] If potential employers think it's important to investigate, how much more do parents need to know what's going on?

Does your child prefer a build-your-own online radio station such as Pandora, last.fm, or Slacker? Are you aware that while he or she could be compiling a list of Christian tunes on that iPhone, it's also easy to access today's sleazy and profane music—sometimes even unintentionally?

Which video games does your child prefer? Does he or she play alone, online, or for untold hours on his or her mobile phone? The fact that gaming's popularity is growing isn't a problem in itself, but it increases the likelihood that our own kids are part of this trend. If so, what are they playing and how much time do they devote to it?

Do you know what Internet sites your children frequent? Millions use the Web to access useful facts and how-to advice, but many kids don't stop there. A study conducted by security firm Symantec Corporation and OnlineFamily.Norton identified the top 100 Internet searches conducted by children. First was YouTube. Fourth was "sex." "Porn" was sixth.[13]

Parents truly have their work cut out for them. Total adult-oriented Internet sites in 2010 numbered 4.2 million—about 12 percent of the Web's total.[14] The National Center for Missing and Exploited Children reports that one in five children ages 10-17 who uses the Internet has been sexually solicited online—and 25 percent have been *unwillingly* exposed to images of nudity. The same organization notes that over the past 10 years there have been nearly 740,000 reports of child sexual exploitation to the federally managed CyberTipline.[15]

Even if your child doesn't view Internet pornography directly, there's plenty of depraved material available on sites like YouTube, where more than one billion videos are watched each day.[16]

Of course, those videos are not all problematic. Some are innocuous, like the one of a man who can draw a near-perfect circle on a chalkboard. Others inspire, such as footage of people rescued from earthquakes and floods. There are educational videos and some very funny clips. And Christians are increasingly using online video for spiritual purposes—at GodTube.com, for example.

But despite the claims of many popular online sites that they don't allow pornography, some wretched stuff lurks there. Near-pornography is routine; even hardcore porn occasionally slips through. YouTube restricts access to some of its most explicit content to those 18 and over, yet it's all too easy for any youngster to lie about age (not that adults should watch that content, either).

Without parental guidance, YouTube can quickly move from family friend to major enemy. So can other popular video sites like video.google.com, video.yahoo.com, vids.myspace.com, and hulu.com.

Do you know what your kids have been watching on the Web? Many parents don't. Forty percent of teenagers say they tell their parents nothing, or virtually nothing, about what they do online.[17]

Many moms and dads also seem to be in the dark when it comes to the old-fashioned way of delivering video—the TV set. The Kaiser Foundation found in a 2010 study that 71 percent of 8-18-year-olds have a TV in their bedroom—and that 68 percent of those kids say their parents have absolutely no rules when it comes to TV viewing.[18] If we want to get technology on our side, we'll need to do better than that.

What to Know #3: Whether Your Child Is a Bully or a Victim
Technology can be a wonderful tool, but it can also introduce a world of hurt—especially when it's a tool for bullies or predators.

It's bad enough that 20 percent of teens admit to having sent risqué photos of themselves via cell phone or e-mail, and that 11 percent of those have sent such photos to complete strangers.[19] It's bad enough when even more—39 percent—say they've sent or posted sexually suggestive e-mails, texts ("sexting"), or instant messages.[20]

But when not-so-friendly peers use their cell phone cameras in locker rooms and other private places, or simply forward revealing photos others have taken, the results can be fatal:

- Jesse Logan, 18, hanged herself in 2008 after a nude picture she'd sent to her boyfriend was forwarded to other high school girls. According to her mother, Jesse began to experience harassment from peers who called her degrading names and threw things at her.[21]
- In 2009, 13-year-old Hope Witsell hanged herself after relentless taunting. She had sent a nude photo of herself to a boy she liked; another girl used his phone to forward it to many of their Tampa, Florida, classmates.[22]

Teens who send inappropriate photos of themselves or others aren't thinking through the repercussions of their actions. Internet safety expert Parry Aftab is concerned about the "digital afterlife" of sexual pictures:

> [Once a picture is sent electronically] it could be in a million places and you never know who got a copy. If you take it on your phone and texted it, a copy exists with your cell phone carrier and on [the recipient's] phone. Maybe he e-mailed it to himself, so now it's on his computer, and if he put it on an SD card and used it on his Xbox, now it's there also. They're also sometimes sold on the digital black market for use on underground websites where real child predators love to look at them.[23]

Cyber-bullying isn't limited to the use of revealing photos. Phoebe Prince, a 15-year-old Irish immigrant, committed suicide in 2010 after being humiliated via text messages and social networking sites. A friend said the "charming" and "pretty" girl had been harassed because others were jealous of her.[24]

Suicide may be a rare response to cyber-bullying, but the bullying itself is disturbingly common. According to a 2007 Pew Research study, almost 32 percent of teens have received threatening messages, had embarrassing photos posted, or seen rumors spread about them online.[25] It's no surprise, then, that in a 2009 Cyberbullying Research Center study, 22 percent of kids reported having participated in online bullying at least twice in the past month.[26]

It's not just an individual sport, either. Juicycampus.com, a now-defunct but once popular Web site, represented 450 schools. It was known for its mean-spirited discussion threads. Subjects ranged from "Smelliest People on Campus" to simply a student's name, followed by the word "discuss"—which often led to free-for-all slams of the person mentioned.[27] More recently, collegeacb.com seemed to inherit the mantle as a clearinghouse for malicious gossip.

Recently we received an e-mail from Holly, who explained how her daughter had been harassed by a former boyfriend using a social networking site:

> She had been seeing a particular boy for over a year, who we inci-
> dentally felt was not a good choice in terms of date material. . . .
> In the past couple weeks, though, we were grateful to hear that
> she had officially broken up with him. However, in angry revenge
> he created a new [MySpace] Web site in her name and wrote all
> sorts of nasty, sensual, and tasteless things, and also included her
> cell phone number and name. After receiving a few phone calls
> and realizing what had happened, she was able to get "his" space
> deleted by the moderator, but she felt very violated by this and
> quite upset.

Bullies aren't the only thugs prowling the Internet, of course. Taking advantage of the anonymity offered by the Web, sexual predators disguise themselves and seek victims.

One such victim was 13-year-old Alicia Kozakiewicz, who disappeared from her Pittsburgh home on New Year's Day, 2002. Her mother, Mary, described herself as "not computer savvy at the time." She didn't think it unusual that Alicia, a shy girl, spent a couple of hours a day on the Internet; when Mary and her husband noticed their daughter using the computer late at night, they accepted her explanations about having forgotten to complete her homework.

They had no idea that Alicia had met a man in a chat room—a 38-year-old divorced computer programmer from Virginia. The man seemed to give her emotional support, even unconditional love.

Eventually he convinced Alicia to meet him. Ironically, he had a daughter her age who had just visited him; after taking his daughter to the airport, he went to Pittsburgh to get his prey.

For four days he kept Alicia chained in his basement, raping and torturing her. He showed video of the assaults to an acquaintance, who called the FBI—fearing he might be arrested as an accomplice.

Alicia was rescued when the FBI broke into her captor's house. The predator was convicted and sentenced to 20 years in prison.

Alicia went on to study psychology and forensics, with the goal of joining the FBI and helping other victims. Along with her parents, she speaks to groups about the potential dangers of the Internet. But as her mother says, "Life is harder for her than it would have been."[28]

What can we learn from this? Alicia's mother suggests helping our kids know the difference between a stranger and a true friend. I agree. But I'd also suggest that a more complete solution may be to steer clear of chat rooms altogether. This doesn't mean prohibiting all high-tech forms of communication, but it does mean limiting their use to staying in touch with real-world friends, acquaintances, and family members.

If you're going to allow your child to visit chat rooms, know who he or she is communicating with and the subjects most often addressed—and regularly look over your child's shoulder to monitor the conversation.

Some may argue that having an edgy social networking profile, carrying on inappropriate online relationships, and flirting in cyber-space are relatively innocent. After all, they're not quite real, are they? But for some young people—especially those who feel under-appreci-ated and under-respected—the anonymity of the Web allows people to lie and otherwise communicate in ways they wouldn't think of doing face-to-face. Our kids need to know that the same values that apply to real-life relationships—respect, integrity, honesty, compassion, and purity—apply online.

What to Know #4: What the Experts Advise

In 2009, Jason Sands of Montana got a 14-year-old girl's phone num-ber from her MySpace account and began sending her "sexts." Fortunately, this girl knew what to do. She gave these messages to her mother, who went to the authorities.

I spoke with Detective Chris Shermer, who took over the Sands case once it came to the attention of law enforcement. Posing as "Kayla," a 14-year-old, Shermer began texting Sands.

Shermer explained to me that laws regarding enticement kept him from initiating any conversations of a sexual nature. But it wasn't long before Sands' texting took a sexual turn. After Sands set up a rendez-vous at the girl's middle school, he was nabbed.

I asked Detective Shermer what advice he would give parents about dealing with predators. He outlined four points:

1. Learn what your kids know. Get up-to-date with the electronics they're using. Sit down and ask, "What are you doing here?"

2. Have the computer out in the open when they're younger.

3. When they're older and need a laptop for homework, have a contract in place. Explain to them, "Here are the rules," such as, "You will always let me see what you post. If I come into your room and you slam shut your laptop, I will [be checking]."

4. Know who your children are really talking to on their cell phones. Consider using a cell phone carrier who will block your child from receiving text messages during school hours (or any hours you set).

We can learn from the experience and training of experts like Detective Shermer. Keep up with their current advice through books, articles, and Web sites like pluggedin.com. And let your kids know that when they get inappropriate texts, tweets, instant messages, or e-mails—maybe even from a "friend" at school—they shouldn't ignore it. They should pass these along to you. As long as people get away with misusing technology, they'll continue. When they have to face the music, they often stop—sometimes as a result of getting arrested.

What to Know #5: The Helpful Side of Technology

While technology can be a foe, it can also be a great family friend. In fact, I believe some of today's technological marvels are almost must-haves for the home. Safeguarding our kids has become much easier because of these modern wonders, with many other helpful gadgets coming right around the corner. Here are three already on the market:

- *The DVR.* As I've already mentioned, there's the digital video recorder. At this writing, only 40 percent of U.S. homes have this device.[29] I wish the number could be 100 percent. Surprisingly, even among those who own one, research shows most don't use it to its full potential. For instance, 40 percent of DVR owners still watch commercials.[30] Personally, I like the way I can zip through an entire four-hour football game in less than half that time. What a time-saver!

  The DVR also allows families to watch at their convenience instead of the network's. More importantly, you can choose to use it to record only positive programming that meets a healthy family standard.

- *The ClearPlay machine.* This device, available at many Christian bookstores and focusonthefamily.com, allows families to rent or buy off-the-shelf DVD movies and some television series, then view them with offensive content edited out. Editing updates for the latest movie releases are provided online at ClearPlay.com for a modest monthly fee. See the interview at the end of this chapter for more about this invention.

- *Internet filters.* The Internet can help your daughter study for her final exam. It can help your son improve his high-jump form for track. But since it also offers millions of inappropriate sites, a growing number of families are using Internet filtering products.

Most of these software systems search the Web and restrict access to sites with problematic content. Several products also notify parents when attempts have been made to access such sites, or when unsuitable e-mails have been attempted. (See focusonthefamily.com/parenting/protecting_your_family/articles/family_safety_resources.aspx for more information. To find out about one particular system, BSecure® Online, go to focusonthefamily.com/bsecure.)

I, for one, am glad when technology comes alongside to help me rather than hurt. I appreciate being able to call roadside assistance when I get a flat tire because I carry a cell phone. I like being able to flash through television commercials using my DVR. I count it a privilege to watch a movie with offensive content edited.

And I love it when I hear tech stories like Dan Woolley's. An employee of Compassion International, Woolley was in the Hotel Montana in Port-au-Prince during the Haitian earthquake of 2010. Trapped in an elevator shaft, he used an iPhone application to learn how to treat the excessive bleeding from cuts on his legs and the back of his head. He also used the light from his phone to properly diagnose his foot as broken, while looking up ways to keep from going into shock. The result: He survived what eventually totaled 65 hours beneath the rubble.[31]

Even social networking can be a wonderful tool. One of my colleagues, Bob Hoose, blogged this:

> According to a *mirror.co.uk* article, a woman named Frances had spent her whole life looking for her estranged dad. Then out of the blue, while researching her family tree, a friend discovered that the 51-year-old Frances had a previously unknown teenage half sister. And wouldn't you know it, Frances spotted this newly discovered sibling's name on Facebook and decided to send her a message.
>
> "This will be a bit of a shock," Frances wrote. "But I think I'm your sister."
>
> The half sis was equally blown away and wrote back: "Do you want to talk to my dad? He's sitting right next to me."
>
> After picking up her teeth (I'm not sure she actually dropped them, but wouldn't you?), Frances started chatting with her dad on Facebook and, that weekend, they met each other again after 48 years apart.[32]

Recently I received an e-mail from Matt, a young Canadian who explained how one advancement in technology (the ability to capture an entire TV series on DVD) has been a real help in providing family-friendly alternatives for himself and his father. He wrote:

My Dad and I don't watch much of the new TV shows currently out as the moral level of most of them isn't great.

Buying TV DVD sets have been a great blessing to us as we've re-watched old favourites of mine like *Home Improvement, Full House, Saved by The Bell, Early Edition, Star Trek, Star Trek: The Next Generation, Star Trek Voyager,* and older favourites that my Dad introduced me into like *The Cosby Show, Family Ties, Get Smart, Mork and Mindy, Andy Griffith, I Love Lucy,* and *Hogan's Heroes.*

I'm very glad for technology that allows me to go back in time in essence and watch the old good shows when current TV fails to provide good content!

One of the more interesting uses of technology I've heard of involved an Israeli university student who opened a Twitter site where prayers can be sent. He promised to place those requests in the crevices of Jerusalem's Western Wall. "I take their prayers, print them out, and drive to Jerusalem to put them in the Western Wall," said Alon Nir, a resident of Tel Aviv.[33]

Technology can be a friend to your clan as well. I hope that in the future we'll see an even greater array of devices, gizmos, and software designed to safeguard our children—rather than exposing them to harmful images and other unhealthy content.

Being Brave in the Brave New World

Space doesn't allow me to list all the ways in which technology delivers information and entertainment, whether beneficially or otherwise. The important thing is that your child shouldn't be wandering through the potential land mines without your regular oversight and involvement. And you don't have to provide that guidance without the help of technology itself. For updated reports on how the latest media and machinery might affect your family, go to pluggedin.com.

Many of us wish we could go back to simpler times free of televisions, computers, theaters, Twitter, cell phones, Second Life, Xboxes,

Facebook, and Wii systems—but we know that will never happen. We can only press ahead, doing our best to get involved in our children's tech world, social networking sites, and other forms of communication and entertainment—making sure they understand that their use of technology needs to mirror the virtues and sensitivity of Jesus.

As author, speaker, and radio host Dr. Jim Burns, founder and president of HomeWord, put it:

> For most of mankind's history, major technological advances came relatively slowly compared to today. The wheel. Bronze. The printing press. Steam locomotive. Cotton gin.
>
> But beginning with the turn of the 20th century, technological advancements such as radio, television, talking pictures, early computers, and calculators were invented and brought to market in seemingly rapid succession. In fact, most products and delivery methods came so quickly into the mainstream that questions about how to handle the moral implications took a backseat.
>
> It's likely that this onslaught of products, inventions, and delivery methods will only exponentially increase as the days march by. As this happens, our lives will be further enriched in many ways. But with these advances will also come new ways for consumers to be tripped up morally, and enticed down pathways that will appeal to our baser instincts.
>
> The solution to the potential negative aspects is not to run and hide, or move to some isolated Pacific island. It's to prayerfully and "Christianly" use technology and technological advances to better ourselves, our families and the Kingdom, and reject the darker sides these advances will no doubt bring our way. It won't necessarily be easy. But for those who successfully learn how to navigate, it will be an important step in greater Christian maturity.[34]

A Chat with ClearPlay's Founder, Bill Aho

Have you ever wished your family could watch a cleaned-up version of a popular movie? So has Bill Aho. Which is why he created ClearPlay, a multifaceted filtering system that redefines "edited for television" by giving parents more control over movie content. While he was still president of the company, I talked with Aho about the technology and his run-ins with Hollywood.

Q: Is ClearPlay your attempt to clean up entertainment?

Bill: People love movies. They're an important part of our culture. But often there's content in them that makes us uncomfortable, particularly with the whole family viewing together. How many times have you heard somebody say, "It was a great movie except for . . ." And how many times have you sat around with your kids watching a DVD, and everybody winces when that one little scene comes on or a couple of those words slip through? We thought people ought to be able to watch movies in their living rooms without that kind of discomfort.

Q: Is it fairly easy to use?

Bill: We give you a little USB FilterStik that goes in your computer. With one click of the mouse, you download all the filters. Then just put it in your DVD player and you're ready to go. It'll hold your settings from film to film until you change them.

Q: Did passage of the 2005 Family Movie Act legitimize the ClearPlay concept?

Bill: That was tremendous news for ClearPlay and a real victory for families. That legislation confirmed what we've always felt: that it's acceptable for families in the privacy of their homes to skip or mute extreme violence, sex, nudity, or

language with the help of technology that lets you prepro-
gram a regular DVD to your personal tastes. We give parents
over 16,000 possible permutations for any given movie, so the
filter settings are very adaptable.

Q: Is it true that now you're filtering some television
shows, too?

Bill: We've done quite a few: *Lost, Scrubs, 24, Heroes, The
Sopranos*, and the first three seasons of *The Office*. There are
more coming all the time. We try to do the most popular TV
series that are available on DVD.

Q: Creative people don't like to see their work tampered
with. Did the studios and their lawyers try to stop you?

Bill: Hollywood decided to sue everybody in [our] industry. When we talked to the studios, they all felt the same
way—that the idea of making copies of movies and selling
them in a jacket with a little E for editing was not something they were comfortable with. Of course, that wasn't our
approach. The directors didn't like what we were doing either,
but they all recognized that ClearPlay is different, because the
editing happens in your home. It's like a magical remote control. So we took that to the courts and urged them to treat us
and think about us very differently.

Q: Differently than, say, an editing service that physically
alters the actual video or DVD?

Bill: That's right. ClearPlay does not create a separate version any more than I create a new song when I listen to a CD
with my own equalizer settings. The courts agreed, so they gave
it a closer look. At the same time, we went to Washington and
talked to our senators and congressmen and asked, "Shouldn't
there be some relief on this? Isn't this simply a case where the
copyright law has not kept pace with technology?" That happens all the time. And they agreed. They said the copyright law
shouldn't outlaw something like this, and in fact they didn't
think that it did. So they said, "Let's clarify the copyright act."
They re-wrote the law to create the Family Movie Act, and the

President signed it. The judge said, "Well, I guess that takes care of ClearPlay," and threw out all claims against us. We haven't had any problems with Hollywood since.

Q: What about companies that do alter films?

Bill: The courts turned their attention toward those groups and ruled against the practice of physically editing movies. That change in the law forced CleanFlicks out of business, though less reputable companies are still out there making copies of DVDs, hoping they don't get caught.

Q: Can you tell us about the process your staff goes through when cleaning up a movie?

Bill: We have a team of six filter developers. We also have a QA department for quality assurance. Once we create a filter, we run it through QA, and they look at a lot of areas to make sure we caught everything. They also check to see that it's smooth. Was it the kind of [cut] that, in most cases, the customer won't even notice? Finally, did we do a good job artistically? Did it all make sense? Was the integrity of the story line maintained, and was it an enjoyable viewing experience? Often it will go through QA and we'll run it through filter development again, making changes until we have a product we feel people are really going to enjoy.

Q: Are there films you won't edit?

Bill: If a film is so content-laden that we can't do a very good job and produce a smooth, satisfactory experience, then we won't do it. It really is an art. People think [the result] is going to be jumpy or choppy, but then they watch it and go, "Wow!" That's what we're after.

[Note: At this writing, ClearPlay technology is available only if using a ClearPlay DVD player. Downloading filters for new movies requires an additional monthly or annual fee. For more information, go to focusonthefamily.com/clearplay or clearplay. com. For additional customer reviews, visit sites like amazon. com or epinions.com.]

ten

Reaching Out to Other Families

Not long ago I spoke by phone with a concerned mother who wanted some advice. "Sallee" explained that she felt helpless to do anything as she watched her son and his two closest friends change from happy elementary kids to gloomy high schoolers with a fascination for the dark side. Not only were these boys fans of deeply problematic bands, but they further identified with these groups by wearing their T-shirts.

"Yesterday," she said, "when I drove the boys to school, I heard them discussing these bands, proud to be their fans." One of the boys, said Sallee, *boasted* that a classmate had referred to him as "too dark."

"I've known one of these boys since the third grade," said Sallee. "Now his hair is long and greasy. He's really getting into this dark image." Her question: "I know the mothers of these boys quite well. And I'm sure they don't realize what their sons are into. What should I do—or should I do nothing?"

There are no quick fixes, but I believe there are some steps Sallee needs to take. I applaud her for calling and being concerned enough to make an effort—not just for her son's sake, but for his friends.

There are a lot of Sallees out there, and a lot of kids like her son. I've talked to many of them. They're your neighbors. They're your cousins. They sit next to you in church. They play on your kids' soccer team. They may even be *you*.

So what should you do when you know a Sallee—or a Sallee's child? Can you and your family make a difference in the lives of others, even when it comes to making media choices? That's what this chapter is about.

Ten Steps to Reaching Out

If you know a family that's suffering stress over entertainment issues, consider the following 10-step approach.

1. *Do something.* This is often difficult—sometimes extremely so. But it's always best to, at the very minimum, *try* to rescue kids. They ultimately belong to God—they're just on loan to us.

2. *Be a conduit of information.* Sallee was sure her friends didn't realize how dark the music was that their sons were into. Should she tell them? Yes. I suggested she invite the moms over and bring up the subject over a cup of coffee. Some parents may not really want to know what their kids are into ("If I know I'll have to deal with it"), but most would appreciate a friend who cares enough to dispense necessary information and the tools to act on it. As Hosea 4:6 says, "My people are destroyed from lack of knowledge."

3. *Never be judgmental.* If Sallee speaks with these mothers and comes across as pointing a finger of blame, she will have failed in her mission. Statements like "I think your sons are being a bad influence on mine" will only close the door to meaningful discussion.

4. *Communicate with love as your main motivation.* If Sallee explains to the moms (as I encouraged her to do) that she cares about her son *and* their sons, she'll deflect negative assumptions about other possible motives (the transfer of guilt, concern just about her son, etc.). It was obvious that Sallee cares deeply about all three of these boys, and needs to express that.

5. *Consider the deeper problems.* Lack of media discernment is a symptom of a deeper issue—like not having a radical, sold-out relationship with God. When teens raised in caring homes gravitate to the dark side, it's usually not just due to curiosity about dark media. As 1 John 1:6 says, "If we claim to have fellowship with him yet walk in the darkness, we lie and do not live by the truth."

Why do young people wallow in the gloom? Look for factors such as poor self-esteem; rejection by peers or a close family member; a father who's absent, distant, or overly critical; lack of spiritual meaning and purpose; sexual abuse; or a spiritually hypocritical home life ("We must don our everything-is-fine image for church"). Use the symptom of poor media discernment as a bridge to the underlying turmoil.

6. *Enlist professional help when necessary.* Clergy and/or professional counselors may be necessary in some cases. This doesn't have to be a last resort, either; it can be, and sometimes should be, one of the very first steps we take.

7. *After talking to the parents, talk to the kids.* Again, express how much you care for them. Tell them what you've seen and heard. Then listen. Ask questions. Listen some more. Ask about the deeper issues ("How are you doing with your relationship to God?" "Is there something that's triggered this interest in the dark side?" "Is there anything we can do to help you find joy in things like light, love, and the good news about Jesus?")

8. *Bring dad into the picture.* I've spoken to many, many mothers over the years regarding their concerns for children who've gone astray. Nine times out of ten, the moms feel they must deal with this issue without much support from Dad; often his lack of involvement is a big part of the problem.

But I believe it's never too late to bring dads into the picture. If a father communicates that he loves his child and is willing to get involved to a significant degree (the child will have ideas on what that means), the family can move toward ultimate healing.

Some fathers just need to be shaken out of their complacency: "Jim, our son told me yesterday that he listens to dark music because he resents how you never say anything to him unless it's critical and condescending. He said he would love to have a weekly breakfast with you to help him feel that he matters to you."

9. *Be patient.* Most children involved with offensive entertainment didn't get there overnight. Most won't come out of the darkness overnight, either. They need a steady, loving presence that repeatedly communicates, "I care. I love. I'll be here for you."

10. *Always be "prayed up."* Lives can't be changed spiritually without the power of the Holy Spirit, which is activated by prayer. Pray before, during, and after talking to these parents. Pray for the young people involved. Ask for wisdom.

Ask God to help you demonstrate and communicate as Jesus would. Isaiah 61:1 tells us that one of the reasons Jesus came was to "proclaim freedom for the captives" and to see "release from darkness for the prisoners." That's your mission, too.

A Media Meeting

Maybe you're thinking, *This would work well if my kids were into unhealthy entertainment along with their friends, but that's not the case.* Is there something you can do to share the "media discernment gospel" without being overbearing? I'd suggest the following.

Consider organizing a meeting of the parents of your children's friends with the purpose of discussing entertainment boundaries. You might use food (like a potluck meal or sharing desserts) to get everyone there.

Don't worry about being a polished speaker. You might want to introduce the subject by saying something like this (but in your own words):

> Thanks for coming tonight. I've been reading a book on media discernment and the way entertainment can influence us. I'm more convinced than ever that entertainment can be a friend or a foe of our kids. I'm also convinced that our job as parents could be a whole lot easier if we could unite on behalf of our children and set some basic boundaries we can all agree on. I know that not all of us will draw these boundaries in the same place. That's okay. But I was wondering if tonight we could settle a few things. Maybe we could agree to . . .
>
> - Encourage our children to avoid the worst forms of entertainment (such as music, TV, movies, video games, and Web sites that are excessively violent or perverse, pro-drug, or occultic).
> - Commit to caring about each other's children as well as our own (and praying for them if the group is so inclined).
> - Respect and uphold your family entertainment standards when your child visits my home, and vice versa.

- Communicate with each other if we have issues that arise over entertainment.
- Commit to knowing what types of media our kids are consuming.
- Respect each other's differences regarding how we settle on media boundaries, realizing some of us will be more strict, some more permissive.

Sending the Message at Church

As I've already mentioned, it's important if you're a Christian to encourage your youth pastor and senior pastor to regularly address the topic of honoring Christ with your entertainment choices. That's true not just for the benefit of your own kids, but other families, too.

It's great when our kids hear our own views and concerns on this subject; in fact, it's the most important thing we can do to reinforce media savviness. But there's nothing like the power of hearing it from the pulpit or within the youth group to help reinforce the concept.

The more it's mentioned during worship services, the more likely others in your circle of friends will also embrace it. Many pastors may need a little nudge in this direction because it's often not on the top of their list of favorite subjects to preach. Avoid nagging, of course; passing along an occasional review, quote, or article from pluggedin.com might serve as a gentle reminder.

Spreading the Word at School

When I teach on the subject of media discernment, I prefer to talk to Christian groups so that I can apply biblical principles to the message. But I've also spoken to parent-teacher organizations (PTOs) and public schools. It's a bit trickier, but I've found that when I'm unable to mention the Bible, Jesus, or specific scriptural principles, I still can find common ground by encouraging parents to help their children develop character—stressing such virtues as integrity, honesty, purity, and compassion.

Are you part of a PTO? Would this group be open to discussing how today's media often war against the very values the group is trying to instill? If you can't lead such a discussion, perhaps your pastor or youth pastor could—realizing that he or she probably won't be able to bring God into the equation in this setting.

Are your kids in a scouting program? A club? Look for ways to suggest smart media and technology choices as a topic for a meeting.

Besides encouraging discussions, you may want to work for change in your school's media policies. When my daughter made the varsity squad of her school's basketball team, for example, this proud papa spent many hours at away games. Sitting in gym after gym, I frequently noticed before games and at halftime that the PA system blared disgusting tunes from very disturbing artists.

I just didn't get it. For years we've educated our children with the underlying assumption that they learn by hearing, and what they were hearing at sporting events, in the cafeteria, in study hall, and even the classroom was teaching some pretty wretched lessons. One mom even called me for help in ridding her son's school bus of audio-trash.

If this is a problem in your child's school, may I suggest trying to get a policy in place that limits public tunes to those that are more positive? It's quite possible objectionable songs are played only because no one has spoken up. Most adults don't listen closely—and if teens are in charge of the PA system, they're likely to choose whatever's hot on the charts.

This may be as easy as informing your school's administration, citing lyrical examples of what's been playing. I'm convinced that many principals, administrators, and board members would be genuinely concerned if they understood the problem.

One thing they'll want to know, of course, is what alternatives exist. Be ready with a list of positive or neutral tunes that fit the bill (you may want to check out music reviews at pluggedin.com). Maybe sending them a copy of this book and a respectful cover letter would help. You may want to mention that entertainment influences even "good kids," and that playing songs publicly on campus can be construed as a defacto endorsement by administrators of the content and message.

If you find quotes from the musicians that show the destructive messages they send are intentional, share these with school officials. For instance, speaking to French TV channel TF1, singer Lady Gaga stated, "This has been the greatest accomplishment of my life—to get young people to throw away what society has taught them is wrong."[1]

For many young people, their first—sometimes only—exposure to destructive movies and tunes happens at school. Schools should be safe havens. It's not about legislating what your children's classmates can listen to on their own time; it's about sending the message that the adults in charge care enough to set healthy boundaries.

I like what my friend and colleague in the battle for wholesome entertainment, the late Dr. C. DeLores Tucker, once told me: "We're not going to be able to rid it from society. But at least we can keep it from being produced and packaged, celebrated, glamorized, and distributed all across not only America, but across the world, in stores and schools where children have ready access to it."

And speaking of school, your kids might be open to influencing teachers and classmates, too. If your children are on board with the idea of making wiser media choices, you might want to encourage them to spread the message as they complete certain assignments. Is it time for a book report? Why not do one on the importance of being media savvy? For that oral report or debate, perhaps your child could tackle a subject like, "Can the Media Influence?" or "How Far Is Too Far When It Comes to Consuming Entertainment?"

It might be quite eye-opening to the class, the teacher—and even your son or daughter.

Influencing the Wider World

I once got a letter from a young lady who was extremely critical of *Plugged In* magazine. She felt that instead of evaluating movies, music, and television, we should spend our time infiltrating Hollywood. Here's what she wrote:

I am writing in regards to the whole premise of your magazine, *Plugged In*. It is a shame and I am sad that this is a magazine sponsored by Christians for I am a Christian just as your writers claim to be. Your magazine is content to sit back and denounce, castigate, and complain about the television status quo without offering any real solutions.

After several sentences explaining how Jesus would choose to change Hollywood from the inside ("I see Him producing positive films that contain Christian values"), she told us how she planned to make a real difference someday:

> I myself plan on majoring in film and entering Hollywood to show them what a real Christian should be like. [Jesus] was part of the solution and I will strive to emulate Him. Hollywood sees your magazine and shakes their head and rolls their eyes and continues to produce the same shows and films. I wish your magazine could truly be salt and light by encouraging Christians to enter the war zone instead of complaining about it and produce films based on godly principles so that we may replace the evil with good.

I'm pleased that this person wants to better Hollywood by becoming an insider (though she may need to mature a bit first). Ambassadors for Christ are desperately needed in the uttermost parts of the earth. That includes being salt and light and using God's gifts to write creative and insightful scripts, develop uplifting and fun video games, launch positive TV programming, and produce songs that are second to none.

Some may think a young person who feels a call to "minister" has really only a few options such as pastor, youth pastor, or missionary. But I believe God also calls His people to be doctors, lawyers, teachers, politicians, mechanics, and a lot of other things. Every walk of life—including acting, Web design, singing, and video editing—needs dedicated servants who see their "job" as a ministry and calling.

I don't believe that bettering Hollywood from the inside precludes the idea that Christians need to be equipped with information to make wise choices. Because of the letter-writer's criticism, it would be easy for me to dismiss everything she writes; but she does bring up an important point. Gifted Christians are needed in the worlds of entertainment and technology. By becoming the best directors, writers, producers, and inventors this world has ever seen, a few believers could win thousands—even millions.

I hope and pray that if your child feels called to use his or her talents in this way, you'll encourage that. After all, Jesus changed this world by coming down from heaven and becoming an "insider."

Even if you don't have a child who's called in this fashion (and that's probably most of us), we all need to make sure our children see the arts as a mission field in need of talented missionaries who serve as "tent makers." Our kids can help inspire and support their gifted, believing friends in making a difference.

Let It Begin with You

Here's my closing challenge: Would you ask the Lord what He wants you to do about entertainment in your home?

Do you need to make some major changes? Some minor ones? Do you simply need to stay the course?

Are you too permissive? Too legalistic?

Are you more concerned about "sin control" than you are that your children are thriving in their faith and commitment to Christ?

Do you need to enter your child's media world more frequently?

Do you need to set a family media standard or have a written constitution?

If you and your kids tend to fight over these issues, is it time to step back and remember the importance of your relationship?

Would it help to share some of the facts in this book with them? Or do they first need to know how much you care before they'll care how much you know?

Whether the path to peace in your family involves discussing, apologizing, exhorting, forgiving, or seeking a counselor's advice, believe that the path is there. I trust that God will guide you as you make your way down that road, and as you commit to honoring Him with your family's entertainment decisions.

One Woman Who
Made a Difference:
Dr. C. DeLores Tucker

Dr. C. DeLores Tucker was a friend, a fellow crusader against indecent entertainment, a longtime civil rights activist, and a vocal opponent of hateful, misogynist rap music. Here's an interview I had with her before she passed away in 2005. It conveys a passion for the cause, a heart for young people, and offers proof that when it comes to media, one person can influence many others.

Q: Dr. Tucker, it's great to talk with you again. We've both been at this a long time. When did you first take up the charge against salacious rap music?

Dr. Tucker: We've had a great battle going since 1995. That's when I heard from the women of the industry—Dion Warwick, Melba Moore, and others. They cried out for help because they didn't like the fact that our children were getting messages telling them to use drugs, drop out of school, and that called women "b--ches" and "hos." The music was teaching them to be thugs. That's why it's called "gangsta rap"—dress like a gangsta, walk like them, go to jail like them, and die like them. We wanted to stop that, so we took on the industry.

Q: You started with Time Warner?

Dr. Tucker: I've sat on corporate boards, so I decided to buy Time Warner stock. That allowed me to go into the stockholders' meeting and read the dirty lyrics to them. I've always believed that if you take on the largest in the industry, a domino theory goes to work and the rest will fall down. Seeing what was in those songs made me march and even get arrested. We marched in front of stores in Washington, D.C., that sold that music. We said we were gonna close the doors. Well, they closed the doors on us; they put us in jail. But we've had some great victories, too.

Q: Despite arrests, lawsuits, malicious personal attacks, and even death threats, God has honored your efforts.

Dr. Tucker: A young lady who sings my spiritual anthem is Yolanda Adams. She sings, "No matter what you're going through, God is using you. The battle is not yours; it's the Lord's." I'm still very involved in making certain that the airwaves, the media, all forms of entertainment are suitable for young ears and will help them grow into the kind of persons we know they need to be to survive. And not just survive, but live the way God created them to live.

Q: What has kept you going, fighting the same battle year in and year out?

Dr. Tucker: God put this passion in me for Him and for His people. I'm willing to die for both. He keeps me going. I get charged up. I'm not the age of Moses yet. Bob, I can't thank you enough because every time I've needed help, and every time I've needed lyrics or resources, you and your team have been there.

Q: Well, thank you. It's been our pleasure. I wonder, Dr. Tucker, if you could say one thing to the entertainment industry, what would it be?

Dr. Tucker: Remember your own childhood. Remember the messages you received as a child. Then think about those who are living now as children. Make sure God would be pleased with your work.

Dr. Tucker concluded that conversation by insisting, "Anytime you see anyone I need to take on, you let me know." She meant it. But on October 12, 2005, at the age of 78, the battles finally ended as she went home to be with the Lord.

Obituaries labeled her everything from "civil rights pioneer" to "hip-hop antagonist." They recognized her work alongside Dr. Martin Luther King Jr., her tenure as Pennsylvania's Secretary of State, and the fact that she founded the National Congress of Black Women. But I'll remember her as a precious kindred spirit who saw past gender and color to the only thing that mattered: right and wrong. That was her fight. And no sacrifice was too great.

Changing the Channels:
A Chat with Brent Bozell

Each spring many families take a seven-day break from television during TV Turnoff Week (now called Digital Detox Week). With that in mind, I decided to chat about TV with Brent Bozell, founder of the Parents Television Council. We talked about the effect parents could have on media producers.

Q: All media seem to push the envelope. What made you concentrate on TV?

Brent: Entertainment television is the single most powerful cultural force in our society today. If you're concerned about the sewage pouring into our society, you have to look at television and the role it plays. We formed the Parents Television Council in 1995 to build a wall and simply say, "No more."

It was very difficult at first. It was a brand-new concept, and the general belief was that nothing could be done. But then I met [late comedian] Steve Allen. He was my political opposite, and yet we agreed on this issue of entertainment. I remember reading a speech he gave at the Banff Film Festival where he took the industry to task, and I figured he'd do what everyone else does: apologize soon after because it could ruin his career. He didn't. In fact, two weeks later he gave another speech even tougher than the first one. He came onboard as our honorary chairman.

We now have over a million members, and I've found that there are people of all political stripes who agree that something has to be done.

Q: Do you have a specific example of how the PTC has made a difference?

Brent: When *7th Heaven* first aired on the WB, it floundered. It was a very positive family program, but it wasn't getting much of an audience. The head of the WB contacted me and we talked about it. I told him his problem was marketing. He was trying to get people already watching television to turn to that show. I suggested that he pursue an audience that had stopped watching television but could be brought back with a good program. We helped them do a marketing campaign reaching out primarily to the religious right by using Christian radio. Within six months *7th Heaven* was the network's number-one show, where it remained for its 10-year life span.

Q: What concerns you about the way that TV is evolving?

Brent: There's this false notion that in cable you've got 100-150 channels out there, so there's great diversity. Actually, seven companies control approximately 80 percent of everything on cable today. Each owns multiple channels. They also own channels like HBO, so they're constantly moving programming from one network to another. The classic example is *Sex and the City*. What they've done is take out things like obscenities and nude scenes, but the story lines and dialogue remain essentially the same. The themes are just as filthy and immoral as they were on premium channels like HBO. That's a dramatic development.

Q: And now those shows are more accessible to children—as if kids needed more edgy content thrown their way.

Brent: The problem is that you still have this nincompoop idea in Hollywood that if you want to attract a young audience, you must give it something offensive. That goes against 50 years of programming history. What does that tell you they think of the American people? They think society is raunchy and they must be raunchy to attract a raunchy audience. I think society is better than that. Experience tells us when you give people positive, quality programming, it becomes successful programming.

Q: Parents tell us they'd prefer to pay for cable channels à la carte, which makes a lot of sense.

Brent: That's the solution. We introduced that idea two years ago, and I think it will ultimately prevail. It simply says that, when you get your cable bill and you've got 80 channels on there, you ought to be able to pick and choose which ones you want to pay for. But the cable industry has thrown up one roadblock after another. It's interesting that the industry tells us it creates offensive programming because that's what people want. If that's true, they'd have no problem with à la carte cable. But it's not true, and they know it. How many parents, given the opportunity, would pay for their children to watch MTV? How many want to pay for an FX network that features the gruesome sadomasochism of *Nip/Tuck*? Not many.

Q: How will the Internet change the television landscape over the next five years?

Brent: Dramatically. So much so that we won't recognize TV as we know it today. The change will be that revolutionary. Time Warner has announced a massive new programming initiative on the Internet. And with the advent of broadband programming, the advertising industry is realizing that it doesn't have to pay massive amounts of money on network or cable to reach a fraction of their targeted audience. Now they can reach viewers online more effectively for a lot less money. Therefore, I predict advertising dollars will shift overwhelmingly to the Internet in the next five years and the broadcast networks will become dinosaurs. Cable will also be threatened as more and more programming shows up online. The Internet is the future, not television.

Q: In the meantime, what steps can families take to clean up TV?

Brent: If the Focus on the Family constituency alone were to stand up and say to advertisers, "I will not buy your product if you underwrite offensive programs," or told broadcasters, "I will protest to the FCC as an owner of the public airwaves every time you violate my community standards," or lobbied Congress to support à la carte cable, we would be successful across the board overnight. I'm not exaggerating. That's how important and powerful Focus on the Family supporters are.

notes

Chapter 1

1. *The Barna Report 1992-1993: An Annual Survey of Life-Styles, Values and Religious Views*, Barna Research Group, 1992.
2. "Teens and Media: Do Christian Teens Behave Differently?" a study conducted by Front Porch Entertainment, February, 2011.
3. Mariel Concepcion, "T.I. Speaks Out Against Gun Violence," Billboard.com, May 12, 2009.
4. "The Buzz (Publick Occurences): Need to Know News," *World* magazine, April 25, 1998. Found at http://www.worldmag.com/articles/1959.
5. Devon Thomas, "Britney Spears Would Lock Her Boys Up 'Until They Turned 30' if They Ever Wanted Fame," CBSNews.com, July 7, 2010. Found at http://www.cbsnews.com/8301-31749_162-200 09872-10391698.html.
6. Dan Rather, *48 Hours*, CBS News, July 5, 2000.
7. President Barack Obama, "We Need Fathers to Step Up," *Parade* magazine, June 21, 2009. Found at http://www.parade.com/export/sites/default/news/2009/06/barack-obama-we-need-fathers-to-step-up.html.
8. David Crowley, "The Original Player," *Vibe* magazine, July 2001. Found at http://books.google.com/books?id=1CUEAAAAMBAJ&pg=PA108&dq=hugh+hefner+vibe+magazine+I+knew+my+mother+loved+me,+but+she+never+expressed+it,+so+I+learned+about+love+from+the+movies&ei=3TatTPX8JIbKzASR46n7CA&cd=1#v=onepage&q&f=false.
9. Michael Medved, "Saving Childhood," *Imprimis*, September 1998. Found at http://www.hillsdale.edu/news/imprimis/archive/issue.asp?year=1998&month=09.
10. Parents Television Council, "TV Bloodbath: Violence on Prime Time Broadcast TV: A PTC State of the Television Industry Report," by

Parents Television Council. Found at http://www.parentstv.org/ptc/publications/reports/stateindustryviolence/main.asp.

11. Paul Asay, "I Can Do Interviews All by Myself," Plugged In Online, September 21, 2009. Found at http://www.pluggedin.com/upfront/2009/icandointerviewsallbymyself.aspx.

12. Sarah Netter, "Former Justice Pushing for More Civics, Less 'American Idol': Sandra Day O'Connor Says Civics Lessons Have All but Vanished," ABC News, March 4, 2009. Found at http://abcnews.go.com/GMA/story?id=7004234&page=1.

13. Meg Shannon, "Popular Children's Web Site Under Attack by Identity Thieves," Fox News, July 9, 2009. Found at http://www.foxnews.com/story/0,2933,530684,00.html?mep.

14. Douglas Gresham, *Focus on the Family* daily radio broadcast, May 7, 2008.

15. Stephen King, "Do Movies Matter (Part 2)," *Entertainment Weekly*, February 1, 2007. Found at http://www.ew.com/ew/article/0,,5468 28,00.html.

16. Steve Knopper, "Reviewer critiques pop music in terms of family values," *Chicago Tribune*, April 11, 2003. Found at http://www.knopps.com/CTPluggedIn.html.

17. E. Stanley Jones, *Victorious Living* (New York: The Abingdon Press, 1938).

Chapter 2

1. Bill Gorman, "2011 Super Bowl XLV Ad Time 90% Sold At $3 Million / 30 Sec.," September 17, 2010. Found at http://tvbythenumbers.com/2010/09/17/2011-super-bowl-xlv-ad-time-90-sold-at-3-million-30-sec/63921.

2. Jason Kovar, "Hollywood's Mission," *Hollywood Unmasked*, 2009. Found at http://www.hollywoodunmasked.com/hollywoodsmission.html.

3. The Rand Corporation, "RAND Study Finds Adolescents Who Watch a Lot of TV with Sexual Content Have Sex Sooner," September 7, 2004. Found at http://www.rand.org/news/press/04/09.07.html. Also The Associated Press, "Dirty song lyrics can prompt early teen sex," August 7, 2006. Found at http://msnbc.com/id/14227775/?GT1=840 4&print=displaymode=1098.

4. The University of North Carolina at Chapel Hill, "Carolina-led Study Examines Sexual Content of Several Media, Affect on Teens'

Sexual Behavior," April 3, 2006. Found at http://www.unc.edu/news/archives/mar06/teenmedia033006.htm.

5. Sharon Jayson, "Study: Drinking, R-rated films linked in middle-schoolers," *USA Today*, April 26, 2010. Found at http://www.usatoday.com/news/health/2010-04-26-rmovies26_ST_N.htm.

6. Brian Stelter, "Report Ties Children's Use of Media to Their Health," *New York Times,* December 1, 2008. Found at http://www.nytimes.com/2008/12/02/arts/02stud.html?_r=1.

7. Cathy Lynn Grossman, "Churches making mainstream films to attract souls," *USA Today*, July 19, 2010. Found at http://webcache.googleusercontent.com/search?q=cache:a9recYMwCXoJ:www.usatoday.com/news/religion/2010-07-19-churchmovies19_CV_N.htm+Movies+are+the+stained-glass+windows+of+the+21st+century,+the+place+to+tell+the+Gospel+story+to+people+who+may+not+read+a+Bible&cd=1&hl=en&ct=clnk&gl=us.

8. "Help Give 'Jesus' to Everyone, Everywhere . . . and Change Lives for Eternity," The Jesus Film Project, 2010. Found at http://www.jesusfilm.org/.

9. Mark Earley, "Bella Babies," *BreakPoint*, December 10, 2008. Found at http://www.breakpoint.org/commentaries/1949-bella-babies.

10. "Child Alerts Family to Fire Because Barney Told Her To," *Orlando Sentinel*, October 21, 1993. Found at http://articles.orlandosentinel.com/1993-10-21/news/9310210572_1_barney-purple-dinosaur-danielle.

11. Associated Press, "Nine-year-old Grayson Wynne, lost in Utah Wilderness, credits survival with TV's 'Man vs, Wild,'" *NY Daily News*, June 23, 2009. Found at http://www.nydailynews.com/news/national/2009/06/23/2009-06-23_nineyearold_grayson_wynne_lost_in_utah_wilderness_credits_survival_with_tvs_man_.html.

12. Bob Smithouser, "Mind Over Media," *Focus on the Family* magazine, April 2001.

13. *Denver Post* Wire Report, "Game inspired teens' spree," *Denver Post*, June 27, 2008. Found at http://www.denverpost.com/search/ci_9712609.

14. AFP, "Thailand bans Grand Theft Auto after taxi driver killing," August 5, 2008. Found at http://afp.google.com/article/ALeqM5i_GdR3NRdfBh-ZIwSv_1vKBE3EUg.

15. Robert F. Howe, "Deadly Games," *Reader's Digest*, August 2005. Found at http://www.rd.com/your-america-inspiring-people-and-stories/ video-game-violence/article27207-1.html.

16. Susan Arendt, "The Dangers of Driving After GTA," Wired.com, May 12, 2008. Found at http://www.wired.com/gamelife/2008/05/ the-dangers-of/#more-7874.

17. CBS News, "2 Guilty of *Scream* Murder," CBSNews.com, July 1, 1999. Found at http://www.cbsnews.com/stories/1999/07/01/ national/main52735.shtml.

18. Alex Mar, "Far from Devil Worship and 'Harry Potter,' Young Witches Explain What They're Really About," MTV News, March 25, 2008. Found at http://www.mtv.com/news/articles/1584096/20080325/ story.jhtml.

19. "Teen 'Twilight' fan charged with making false report in biting incident," *South Florida Sun Sentinel*, February 11, 2011. Found at http://articles. sun-sentinel.com/2011-02-11/news/fl-fantasy-biting-20110211_1_false- report-deputies-marks.

20. Daniel P. Finney, "Teen allegedly bites 11 students; father blames 'Twi- light' movie," *Des Moines Register*, March 27, 2009. Found at http:// pqasb.pqarchiver.com/desmoinesregister/access/1703665601.html?FM T=ABS&date=Mar+27%2C+2009.

21. Xan Brooks, "Natural born copycats," Guardian News and Media Limited, December 20, 2002. Found at http://www.guardian.co.uk/ culture/2002/dec/20/artsfeatures1.

22. Henry Adaso, "Man Kills Wife and Kids, Blames Eminem's Lyrics," About.com, June 23, 2009. Found at http://rap.about.com/b/2009/ 06/23/man-who-killed-wife-and-kids-blames-eminems-lyrics.htm. Also "Eminem's Lyrics Inspired a Fan to Kill," Softpedia.com, December 3, 2005. Found at http://news.softpedia.com/news/ Eminem-s-Lyrics-Inspired-A-Fan-To-Kill-13980.shtml. Also "Articles on Eminem-inspired violence," Thefreeradical.com. Found at http://www.thefreeradical.ca/copycatCrimes/eminemInspired Violence.html.

23. "Avatar-Induced Depression: Coping with the Intangibility of Pan- dora (Video)," The Huffington Post, January 12, 2010. Found at http://www.huffingtonpost.com/2010/01/12/avatar-induced- depression_n_420605.html. Original site Avatar-Forums.com.

24. The Associated Press, "Teen arrested in former mayor's stabbing death," State and Local Wire, March 2, 2003. Found at https://www.nexis.com/research/search.

25. Insane Clown Posse, "Mad Professor," ST Lyrics. Found at http://www.stlyrics.com/songs/i/icp4323/madprofessor202519.html. Warning: contains profanity.

26. Heidi Dawley, "Media as kids' looming s*x super peer," by Heidi Dawley. *Media Life Magazine*, March 22, 2006. Found at http://www.medialife magazine.com/cgi-bin/artman/exec/view.cgi?archive=170&num=3604].

27. Plugged In Online, "Culture Clips," February 15, 2010. Found at http://www.pluggedin.com/cultureclips/2010/2010-02-15.aspx. Quote originally cited at thechurchreport.com, February 8, 2010.

28. Julie Steenhuysen, "Cigarettes in movies seen to cause teen smoking," Reuters, August 21, 2008. Found at http://www.reuters.com/article/idUSN2144036520080821.

29. James D. Sargent, M.D., et al., "Exposure to Movie Smoking: Its Relation to Smoking Initiation Among U.S. Adolescents," *Pediatrics*, November 1, 2005. Found at http://pediatrics.aappublications.org/cgi/content/full/116/5/1183?maxtoshow=&hits=10&RESULTFOR MAT=&fulltext=smoking+in+movies&searchid=1&FIRSTINDEX=0 &sortspec=relevance&resourcetype=HWCIT.

30. "Smoking: Join Joe to Quit Now," WebMD, November 20, 2003. Found at http://www.webmd.com/content/article/77/95433 .htm?printing=true.

31. Mike White, "Making a Killing," *New York Times,* May 2, 2007. Found at http://www.nytimes.com/2007/05/02/opinion/02white .html.

32. Joe Eszterhas, "Hollywood's Responsibility for Smoking Deaths," *New York Times*, August 9, 2002. Found at http://www.nytimes.com/2002/08/09/opinion/09ESZT.html?scp=1&sq=hollywood's%20 responsibility%20for%20smoking%20deaths&st=cse.

Chapter 3

1. The Nielsen Company, "Nielsen Study: How Teens Use Media," June 2009. Republished by Scribd.com. Found at http://www.scribd.com/doc/16753035/Nielsen-Study-How-Teens-Use-Media-June-2009-Read-in-Full-Screen-Mode.

2. Ibid.

3. The Kaiser Family Foundation, "Daily Media Use Among Children and Teens up Dramatically from Five Years Ago," January 20, 2010. Found at http://www.kff.org/entmedia/entmedia012010nr.cfm.

4. Ibid.

5. Patricia McDonough, "TV Viewing Among Kids at an Eight-Year High," Nielsen Wire of The Nielsen Company, October 26, 2009. Found at http://blog.nielsen.com/nielsenwire/media_entertainment/tv-viewing-among-kids-at-an-eight-year-high/.

6. The Kaiser Family Foundation, "Generation M^2: Media in the lives of 8-18 year-olds," January 2010. Found at http://www.kff.org/entmedia/upload/8010.pdf.

7. "Kids watching hours of TV at home daycare," Associated Press, November 23, 2009. Found at http://www.msnbc.msn.com/id/34096613.

8. Richard Louv, *Last Child in the Woods: Saving Our Children from Nature-Deficit Disorder* (Chapel Hill, North Carolina: Algonquin Books, 2008), pp. 1-2.

9. Stan Campbell and Randy Southern, *Mind over Media* (Wheaton, Illinois: Tyndale House Publishers/Focus on the Family, 2001), pp. 153-55.

10. Ibid., pp. 144-45.

11. Sheila Marikar, "'Sex and the City' Fiend: Show Turned Me into Samantha," ABC News Entertainment, May 21, 2008. Found at http://abcnews.go.com/Entertainment/story?id=4895398&page=1.

12. "Lindsay Lohan: 'I Was Irresponsible,'" usmagazine.com, August 31, 2010. Found at http://www.usmagazine.com/moviestvmusic/news/lindsay-lohan-i-was-irresponsible-2010318.

13. Douglas Wilson, "Live or Onscreen, It's Still Voyeurism," Plugged In Online, March 5, 2007. Found at http://www.pluggedin.com/upfront/2007/LiveorOnscreenItsStillVoyeurism.aspx.

14. Maurice Chittenden and Matthew Holehouse, "Boys who see porn more likely to harass girls," *The Times*, January 24, 2010. Found at http://www.timesonline.co.uk/tol/news/uk/crime/article6999874.ece.

15. Janis Wolak, J.D., Kimberly Mitchell, Ph.D., and David Finkelhor, Ph.D., "Unwanted and Wanted Exposure to Online Pornography in a National Sample of Youth." February 5, 2007. Found at http://pediatrics.aappublications.org/cgi/content/full/119/2/247?maxtoshow=&hits=10&RESULTFORMAT=&fulltext=Unwanted+and+Wanted+Exposure+to+Online+Pornography+in+a+National+Sample+of+Youth+

Internet+Users&searchid=1&FIRSTINDEX=0&sortspec=relevance&resourcetype=HWCIT.

16. "'Cool Dad' Hires Stripper for Boy, 12," *Chicago Tribune*, December 20, 1994.

17. Al Menconi, *But It Doesn't Affect Me!* (Carlsbad, California: New Song Publishing, 2004), pp. 123-27.

Chapter 4

1. Jocelyn Vena, "Heidi Montag Says Posing for *Playboy* 'a Huge Honor,'" MTV.com, June 15, 2009. Found at http://www.mtv.com/news/articles/1613996/20090615/story.jhtml.

2. Rob Brendle, *In the Meantime* (Colorado Springs, Colorado: Waterbrook Press, 2005), p. 159.

3. Ibid., p. 164.

4. Tanner Stransky, "A 'Roseanne' Family Reunion," *Entertainment Weekly*, October 24, 2008. Found at http://www.ew.com/ew/article/0,,20235368,00.html.

5. Maria Elena Fernandez, "Just the way you are: 'Ugly Betty's' young nephew has been embraced by those who don't 'fit in,'" *Los Angeles Times*, January 1, 2007.

6. Ramin Setoodeh, "Kings of Queens," *Newsweek*, November 12, 2009. Found at http://www.newsweek.com/2009/11/11/kings-of-queens.html.

7. Cole NeSmith, "The Dangers of Emotional Pornography," *Relevant* magazine, May 10, 2010. Found at http://www.relevantmagazine.com/life/relationship/features/21488-emotional-pornography.

Chapter 5

1. Donald C. Stamps, ed., *The Full Life Study Bible* (Grand Rapids, Michigan: Zondervan Publishing Company, 1992), p. 1944.

Chapter 6

1. "Americans Are Most Likely to Base Truth on Feelings," Barna Group, February 12, 2002. Found at http://www.barna.org/barna-update/article/5-barna-update/67-americans-are-most-likely-to-base-truth-on-feelings.

2. Craig and Janet Parshall, *Traveling a Pilgrim's Path* (Wheaton, Illinois: Tyndale House Publishers/Focus on the Family, 2003), p. 184.

3. Chip Ingram, *Effective Parenting in a Defective World* (Carol Stream, Illinois: Tyndale House Publishers/Focus on the Family, 2006), p. 14.

4. Bob Smithouser, et al., *Movie Nights for Kids* (Wheaton, Illinois: Tyndale House Publishers/Focus on the Family, 2004), p. 144.

5. Joe White and Lissa Halls Johnson, *Sticking with Your Teen* (Carol Stream, Illinois: Tyndale House Publishers/Focus on the Family, 2006), pp. 73-76.

Chapter 7

1. "The Motion Picture Production Code of 1930 (Hays Code)," last updated by Matt Bynum, April 12, 2006. Found at http://www.arts reformation.com/a001/hays-code.html.

Chapter 8

1. Earl Simmons and Anthony Fields, "X Is Coming." Found at http://www.metrolyrics.com/xis-coming-lyrics-dmx.html. Warning: profanity.

2. Eminem, "Role Model." Found at http://www.sing365.com/music/lyric.nsf/Role-Model-lyrics-Eminem/B5A3211B41B0FAF64825688 800111244. Warning: profanity.

3. Alan Light, "Eminem: Behind Blue Eyes," *Spin Magazine,* July 22, 2003. Found at http://www.spin.com/articles/eminem-behind-blue-eyes. Warning: profanity.

4. Liz Perle, "Sneaking into R-Rated Movies (Without Leaving Home)," Common Sense Media, April 14, 2010. Found at http://www.common-sensemedia.org/sneaking-r-rated-movies-without-leaving-home.

5. Dr. Bill Maier, *Focus on the Family Weekend* radio broadcast, August 25, 2007.

6. Liz Szabo, "Report: TV, Internet harm kids," *USA Today,* December 2, 2008. Found at http://www.usatoday.com/news/health/2008-12-01-media_N.htm.

7. Andre Yoskowitz, "Extended TV watching linked to higher risk of death," After Dawn News, January 13, 2010. Found at http://www.afterdawn.com/news/article.cfm/2010/01/14/extended_tv_watching_linked_to_higher_risk_of_death.

8. Liz Szabo, "Study is loud and clear: Teen hearing loss rising," *USA Today,* August 18, 2010. Found at http://www.usatoday.com/print edition/life/20100818/hearing18_st.art.htm.

9. Joe White and Lissa Halls Johnson, *Sticking with Your Teen* (Carol Stream, Illinois: Tyndale House Publishers/Focus on the Family, 2006), p. 76.

Chapter 9

1. Kevin Kelly, "Everything that Doesn't Work Yet," The Technium, February 22, 2007. Found at http://www.kk.org/thetechnium/archives/2007/02/everything_that.php.

2. Dr. Archibald D. Hart, *Sleep, It Does a Family Good* (Carol Stream, Illinois: Tyndale House Publishers/Focus On the Family, 2010), pp. 7-8.

3. Marissa Lang, "Turn off, tune out, turn in: Teens who stay up late, texting and talking, risk daytime health problems," *Sacramento Bee*, July 12, 2009. Found at "Too much texting can deprive teens of zzzs" at http://www.startribune.com/lifestyle/health/53252917.html.

4. "Culture Clips," November 9, 2009. Cited by Plugged in Online from ContraCostaTimes.com. Found at http://www.pluggedin.com/cultureclips/2009/november92009.aspx.

5. Ben O'Brien, "Txting away ur education," *USA Today*, June 23, 2009. Found at http://content.usatoday.com/topics/post/Forum+commentary/68380777.blog/1.

6. "Tech addiction 'harms learning,'" BBC News, September 15, 2009. Found at http://news.bbc.co.uk/2/hi/uk_news/education/8256490.stm.

7. "Teen Tech Use: Too Much, Too Soon?" CBSNews.com, May 25, 2010. Found at http://www.cbsnews.com/stories/2010/05/25/earlyshow/leisure/gamesgadgetsgizmos/main6517203.shtml.

8. Mike Snider, "Nielsen: time spent playing games up," *USA Today*, August 11, 2009. Found at http://content.usatoday.com/communities/gamehunters/post/2009/08/nielsen-time-spent-playing-games-up/1.

9. "The First Thing Young Women Do in the Morning: Check Facebook (Study)," Mashable.com, July 7, 2010. Found at http://mashable.com/2010/07/07/oxygen-facebook-study/.

10. "Hottest June on Record for Video Gaming," Nielsen Wire, August 10, 2009. Found at http://blog.nielsen.com/nielsenwire/media_entertainment/hottest-june-on-record-for-video-gaming/.

11. Bob Hoose with Kevin Simpson, "Halo 3," Plugged In Online, 2007. Found at http://www.pluggedin.com/games/2007/Q4/Halo3.aspx.

12. Christine Roberts, "Hey kids, Facebook is forever," *NY Daily News*, July 14, 2009. Found at http://www.nydailynews.com/money/2009/07/14/2009-07-14_hey_kids_facebook_is_forever.html.

13. "School's Out and Your Kids Are Online: Do You Know What They've Been Searching for This Summer?" Norton Online Family, 2009. Found at http://onlinefamilyinfo.norton.com/articles/schools_out.php.

14. Daniel Weiss, "Children and Pornography Online," *CitizenLink*, June 14, 2010. Found at http://www.citizenlink.com/2010/06/children-and-pornography-online/.

15. Andrew Alexander, "A KidsPost Opening for Predators?" *Washington Post*, October 11, 2009.

16. Michael Arrington, "YouTube Video Streams Top 1.2 Billion/Day," Tech Crunch, June 9, 2009. Found at http://techcrunch.com/2009/06/09/youtube-video-streams-top-1-billionday/.

17. Donna Leinwand, "Survey: 1 in 5 teens 'sext' despite risks," *USA Today*, June 25, 2009. Found at http://www.usatoday.com/tech/news/2009-06-23-onlinekids_N.htm.

18. "Generation M^2: Media in the Lives of 8-18 year-olds," Kaiser Family Foundation, January 2010. Found at www.kff.org/entmedia/upload/8010.pdf.

19. "Sex and Tech: Results from a Nationally Representative Survey of Teens and Young Adults," by The National Campaign to Prevent Teen and Unplanned Pregnancy, conducted September 25 through October 3, 2008. Found at http://www.thenationalcampaign.org/sextech/. Also usatoday.com, June 24, 2009, as quoted in "Culture Clips," Plugged In Online, June 29, 2009. Found at http://www.pluggedinonline.com/cultureclips2/a0004667.cfm.

20. Ibid.

21. Mike Celizic, "Her teen committed suicide over 'sexting,'" *The Today Show*, March 6, 2009. Found at http://today.msnbc.msn.com/id/29546030.

22. Libby Quaid, "Think your kid isn't 'sexting'? Think again," Associated Press, December 3, 2009. Found at http://www.msnbc.msn.com/id/34257556/ns/technology_and_science-tech_and_gadgets/.

23. Gil Kaufmann, "How Can You Avoid Sexting Dangers?" MTV News, February 12, 2010. Found at http://www.mtv.com/news/articles/1631759/20100211/story.jhtml.

24. Pete Kotz, "Phoebe Prince, 15, Commits Suicide After Onslaught of Cyber-Bullying from Fellow Students," True Crime Report, January 28, 2010. Found at http://www.truecrimereport.com/2010/01/phoebe_prince_15_commits_suici.php.

25. Amanda Lenhart, "Cyberbullying," Pew Internet & American Life Project, a Project of the Pew Research Center, June 27, 2007. Found at http://www.pewinternet.org/Reports/2007/Cyberbullying.aspx.

26. Emily Bazelon, "Have You Been Cyberbullied?" Slate.com, January 26, 2010. Found at http://www.slate.com/id/2242666/.

27. ABC News, October 3, 2008, as quoted in "Culture Clips," Plugged In Online.

28. Mary Kozakiewicz, "Mary, a Mother's Story," The Alicia Project, November 30, 2009. Found at http://www.aliciaproject.com/category/aliciaproject/.

29. "Report: Bigger TVs, DVR and Wi-Fi Among Hot U.S. Home Technology Trends," Nielsen Wire, September 30, 2010. Found at http://blog.nielsen.com/nielsenwire/consumer/report-bigger-tvs-dvr-and-wi-fi-among-hot-u-s-home-technology-trends/.

30. "How Teens Use Media: A Nielsen Report on the Myths and Realities of Teen Media Trends," The Nielsen Company, June 2009.

31. Mike Celizic, "Buried in Haiti rubble, U.S. dad wrote goodbyes," The Today Show, January 19, 2010. Found at http://today.msnbc.msn.com/id/34933053/ns/today-today_people/.

32. Bob Hoose, "A Sweet, Salty Facebook Tale," Plugged In Online, January 28, 2010. Found at http://www.focusonlinecommunities.com/blogs/pluggedin/2010/01/28/a-sweet-salty-facebook-tale.

33. Lianne Gross, Jeffrey Heller, and Janet Lawrence, "Twitter site offers followers line to God," Reuters, August 18, 2009. Found at http://www.reuters.com/article/idUSTRE57H1OU20090818.

34. Jim Burns, radio host and founder and president of HomeWord, interview October 1, 2010.

Chapter 10

1. Sheila Marikar, "Lady Gaga Health Issues: Rumor or Reality?" ABC News, May 26, 2010. Found at http://abcnews.go.com/Entertainment/SummerConcert/lady-gaga-rumor-reality/story?id=10738191.

FOCUS ON THE FAMILY®

Welcome to the Family

Whether you purchased this book, borrowed it, or received it as a gift, thanks for reading it! This is just one of many insightful, biblically based resources that Focus on the Family produces for people in all stages of life.

Focus is a global Christian ministry dedicated to helping families thrive as they celebrate and cultivate God's design for marriage and experience the adventure of parenthood. Our outreach exists to support individuals and families in the joys and challenges they face, and to equip and empower them to be the best they can be.

Through our many media outlets, we offer help and hope, promote moral values and share the life-changing message of Jesus Christ with people around the world.

Focus on the Family MAGAZINES

These faith-building, character-developing publications address the interests, issues, concerns, and challenges faced by every member of your family from preschool through the senior years.

For More INFORMATION

 ONLINE:
Log on to
FocusOnTheFamily.com
In Canada, log on to
FocusOnTheFamily.ca

 PHONE:
Call toll-free:
**800-A-FAMILY
(232-6459)**
In Canada, call toll-free:
800-661-9800

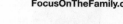

THRIVING FAMILY®	**FOCUS ON**	**FOCUS ON**	**FOCUS ON**
Marriage & Parenting	**THE FAMILY**	**THE FAMILY**	**THE FAMILY**
	CLUBHOUSE JR.®	**CLUBHOUSE®**	**CITIZEN®**
	Ages 4 to 8	Ages 8 to 12	U.S. news issues

Rev. 3/11

More Great Resources
from Focus on the Family®

Essentials of Parenting: Be Prepared
Equipping Kids to Face Today's World
This DVD presents practical plans for dealing with dangers including Internet porn, alcohol, drugs, eating disorders, and premarital sex. You'll see how to resist the impulse to overprotect your child—and gain insights to help you prepare him or her for the world of today and tomorrow.

Movie Nights
By Bob Smithouser
Turn 25 entertaining, thought-provoking films into dynamic opportunities to connect with your kids and help them critically evaluate the media they consume. Each "movie night" features discussion questions, activities, related Scriptures and more. Help young people dissect motion pictures from a biblical perspective—*for life!*

Plugged In Mobile App
Get instant reviews of the latest media releases from a Christian perspective—so you can make the best entertainment choices for your family anytime, anywhere.
www.PluggedIn.com

FOR MORE INFORMATION

Online:
Log on to FocusOnTheFamily.com
In Canada, log on to FocusOnTheFamily.ca

Phone:
Call toll-free: 800-A-FAMILY
In Canada, call toll-free: 800-661-9800

FOCUS® ON THE FAMILY

BPZZXP1